Footsteps into the Light

With dewl Best wisher
from [signature]
1st November 2022

*A Comprehensive Handbook and Practical Guide
into the Spiritual Life for the Enquiring Mind*

*Spirituality and Reality
With an Element of Human Interest*

Thought Provoking Information and Ideas

Living in the 'Now' and the 'Hereafter'

FOOTSTEPS

into the

LIGHT

GEOFF THOMAS

Matador
9 Priory Business Park,
Wistow Road, Kibworth Beauchamp,
Leicestershire, LE8 0RX
Tel: 0116 279 2299
Email: books@troubador.co.uk
Web: www.troubador.co.uk/matador
Twitter: @matadorbooks

ISBN 978 1789015 546

British Library Cataloguing in Publication Data.
A catalogue record for this book is available from the British Library.

Printed and bound in the UK by TJ International, Padstow, Cornwall
Typeset in 12pt Minion Pro by Troubador Publishing Ltd, Leicester, UK

Matador is an imprint of Troubador Publishing Ltd

MIX
Paper from
responsible sources
FSC® C013056

To the Glory of God
Father, Son and Holy Spirit
and
All Who Come In His Name

For
Jacqueline, my late Wife, now in Spirit and
Matthew, my Son and Catalyst come to Earth

There is education, there is learning, there is knowledge. And there is wisdom.

The truth is often simple. It is man that complicates it. The more learned the man, the more complicated it can become.

TRUE OR FALSE?

I didn't ask to be born!

You're only here once!

You're a long time dead!

You only get one life!

You only get old once so you might as well enjoy it!

You can choose your friends but you can't choose your family!

ANSWERS WITHIN

CONTENTS

DIAGRAMS &
ILLUSTRATIONS

ACKNOWLEDGEMENTS

My thanks are extended to family, friends and all on both sides of the great divide who have most kindly provided assistance, encouragement and good wishes in the production of this book.

Acknowledgements are due to the learning establishments, organisations, sole practitioners and churches that I have had the benefit of attending, visiting or being associated with, especially during the years 1988 to 1995, and maintaining connections at varying levels thereafter, especially:

The College of Psychic Studies: The College of Healing

The National Federation of Spiritual Healers (The Healing Trust)

Spiritualist Association of Great Britain: City Literary Institute

The Churches' Fellowship for Psychical and Spiritual Studies

The Christian Spiritualist Society International: Morley College

Spirit Release Societies – BASR and Hickman Academy

Maisie Besant; Margaret Sharland (CPS and Home Circle); Peter McDonnell; David Cousins; Coral Polge; David Chapman

My thanks are extended under this heading to the incumbent Rectors and all at the Church of St Mary-le-Bow in the City of London for the opportunity first granted me in January 1995 to conduct public Spiritual Healing sessions at the Church, followed by Teaching Classes in Healing and Spiritual Development. This led to the founding of the Healing Fellowship in the heart of the Square Mile, the Financial District, for over twenty years altogether.

———————

In the early years, mentioned above, the trunk in the attic of my mind was swiftly unlocked and opened, in the manner of the concept described in chapter 22 – Self Empowerment, bringing about a rapid understanding of stored Esoteric Knowledge and the Ancient Wisdom, as exemplified in a letter at that time from Tony Neate of The College of Healing, viz:

TUTORIAL ASSESSMENT

Geoff Thomas Part 3, November 1989

I must congratulate you on an excellently presented series of comprehensions and essays. What a wonderful 'textbook' for you in time to come.

You have written with eloquence and sensitivity, showing an exceptional understanding of the whole course, and it is with the greatest of pleasure that I recommend you for your Diploma.

Well done, Geoff!

Tony Neate
8.5.90.

(Titles from a selection of books written by Tony are in the Bibliography)

FOREWORD

BY MORVEN FYFE

This book brings into being the teachings of Geoff Thomas who, well knowing his subject, offers to share it with the world. His concept, *Spirituality is Reality,* opens the door to a fascinating exploration, taking the reader on a spiritually uplifting journey that is also helpfully down to Earth. Geoff leaves no stone unturned, and to the reader this will be an intriguing fabric of esoteric knowledge, original thought and spiritual insight, to be found here sometimes in the most unexpected places.

I first met Geoff some twenty-three years ago. It was during my lunch hour that I happened upon a propped up street sign with the words, *'The Laying on of Hands'*; it was sitting on the stone courtyard next to the St Mary-le-Bow church (soon to be mentioned in Chapter 1). As I walked down the narrow steps to the crypt, my curiosity intuited an increasingly warm feeling of welcome. I walked through the open door, and Geoff was standing there to greet me, his face in a relaxed joyful smile, his arms open in a welcoming gesture. Around him were students and trained healers, some already engaged in the laying on of hands with seated members of the public, all in reverent silence. As I stood I was aware that a number of City workers (also in their lunch hour) were assembling into a queue in order to take their turn, sit down and receive something of the same.

I soon found out that Geoff was an adult education teacher who also ran classes at St Mary-le-Bow. These explored processes of spiritual healing and the necessity of understanding all things spiritual. I attended some and always found everyone to be openly animated with fellowship and curiosity. A sense of fun, equality and opportunity abounded; where questions were answered and sensitive matters pertaining to God and the Spirit were respectfully and openly explored.

If ever you've had a favourite teacher or subject, you'll know how your success in that subject rested upon the sheer vitality of the relationship between you and your teacher. A kind of spark happens that alters each one of you, and there have been studies that enthuse about the 'space in between' that connects one to the other. The importance of a realised relationship between people is recognised to be fundamental to progress in educational, medical and mental health endeavours today.

Yet what might be the benefits of a relationship with Spirit, and how can that be realised? Most of us attend funerals and weddings, yet spirituality is a delicate idea that for many people has hardly been touched upon. On matters of religion, the largest percentage of people in our country today call themselves 'spiritual, but not religious'. Should it not be a human right to be able to talk about Spirit without fear of being criticised, or being thought a bit odd? This is where Geoff offers a guiding hand, and points the way in this book, *Footsteps into the Light*.

As elaborated by him, "We are all searching for the Light, even without realising it".

I work in a field where relationship is vital. As a specialised counsellor and psychotherapist, I engage with children and people of all ages who suffer from a variety of conditions and relational traumas. In the media, poor emotional health has become far less of a taboo and, as a society, increasingly there is a listening ear for those who are suffering. There's a greater need for the truth, and it seems we're all developing into more sensitive people. As more people take on the task of improving their physical and emotional well-being, the profession keeps expanding accordingly.

Therefore, perhaps, there is a hole or a hunger for the healing that spiritual connection can give us. Far back, visits to the Church for counsel with God were frequent and, going on to the earliest days of psychoanalysis, the human psyche was called the 'seat of the soul'. Today, it's intriguing that the words, *mind, spirit, psyche, brain and body* are considered separate components. It's rare to find them considered as inseparable within man and woman. Nowadays, bringing in the role of neural science, neural scanning shows us how the brain is altered through relationship with Spirit. I find Geoff's teaching to be refreshingly clear, as for example when he explains:

"The brain is like a processor in the material aspect and the mind, associated with the Spirit, is the creative thought which feeds or serves the processor."

The counselling and psychotherapy professions are increasingly open to this concept, and are enthusiastic about the use of transpersonal and spiritual tools. These are respected because, as research shows, they bring a measurable return of better health. Helpers of the suffering may well find clarity and support for their understanding as they go through this book.

In the wider world, I feel there is a need for 'the man in the street' to know, be able to connect, and support the self and others through knowledge of the structures of spiritual experience and understanding. Geoff's book offers a map and the wherewithal to find these structures of understanding to the soul's journey and, similarly, he brings into relevance the energy and sense of knowing that can easily lie dormant within.

Are there opportunities of further development between man and Spirit and God? It's apparent that 'Spirit' in the form of a higher love is being sought by humankind all over the world.

Geoff shows us the stepping stones that we need to understand about Spirit in order to navigate and evolve to the next level. He recognises this leaning towards relationship with Spirit as being nothing new, and it is something that Geoff explores fearlessly as a necessity in this age.

This book is indeed a wondrous fruition of a lifetime

of questions and answers in the realm of faith, healing and spiritual development. I convey it to the reader as a seeker, that you may find that which is of a healing nature to yourself, your family and friends.

Morven Fyfe (mbacp) M.A., Dip. Couns. (Accred.)

PREFACE

Welcome to the world of spirituality and reality, which among an array of fascinating topics in cosmology and evolution, parapsychology, metaphysics and the paranormal, together with the wisdom of the Good Book, is one deserving to be brought more readily to the attention of a wider and general readership than the more erudite teachings available for the student and the specialist.

There are many excellent teaching books, of course, for the beginner, intermediate and advanced, but it is part of my teaching philosophy to offer ideas and information in a simple, straightforward and collective way so that they can reach the farthest corners of human receptivity as is reasonably possible.

It is my intention that this book will provide comfortable reading for the enquiring mind and be available and of interest for all levels of understanding; humankind's guide to its remarkable place in the order of things. It is a concise guide drawn from my innate understanding, philosophy and learning of the life eternal, together with my teaching and working practice carried out over many years in the world in which we now live and is focussed, essentially, on spiritual realisation, spiritual development and spiritual healing – in fact, spiritual reality.

Each chapter has a clear and defined subject heading, taking the reader forward from one level of understanding to another. It will be found that due to the interacting nature of the subject matter as a whole – which is gradually being drawn together – some aspects of a particular chapter may re-appear in another chapter having a completely different heading.

There are instances, too, where surprising and interesting topics, seemingly unaligned at first to any of the subject headings, have been introduced. There is something for everyone, whether travelling, starting or waiting to begin their journey on the fascinating and inclined eternal pathway; all helping to lead one forward on life's incredible journey, so easily and often accomplished without possibly ever knowing the real reason for why we've been here.

I do not set out to prove anything to you but to inform. I invite readers to reach out and accept the hand of spiritual knowledge and understanding offered them. If what is said in this book resonates with your level of thinking, then I say 'Hold on to it'. If it should be otherwise, then 'hold on to your own truth' – it is important to you.

There is much discussion these days about the reduction in religious following and church attendances, as well as about interfaith, multi-faith and secular societies. A number of people describe themselves as 'spiritual but not religious'.

An explanation of spiritual reality on offer here in the form of a step by step guide surmounts such concerns, concentrating, as it does, strictly on the relationship between humankind and its maker and the wider world considerations extending beyond many a person's everyday way of life – but ones which affect and occupy the greater part of their infinite life than might be supposed.

The author is Christian and uses Christian narrative to explain a point. As with all his work in the spiritual field he invites all faiths to this book, as well as to any without faith or belief. The truth is for all; it is universal.

Happy reading.

Geoff Thomas
London, 2018

Blessed are they that have not seen, and yet believed

John: 20.29

1

INTRODUCTION

Driving westward along the M4 motorway on the stretch between London and Reading on an otherwise peaceful April evening in 2015 after the peak of the traffic rush hour had eased, I switched on the car radio to listen to a regular half-hour science programme. Comfortably settled while the car was moving I was aware that several topics were being discussed in what I sometimes term a kaleidoscopic presentation – a bit of this and a bit of that. All was uneventful for me until the presenter, evidently a man of science, began to talk about dark matter (in the universe), and to illustrate a point he suggested that listeners might imagine a ghost passing through a solid wall, hastily adding, "If you believe that sort of thing."

A most inoffensive remark to most listeners, no doubt, but I was immediately alerted. Here we go again were my thoughts! What the presenter thought to himself and to what extent he was advised to add that discretionary disclaimer I know not but the fact that it had been inserted was evidence again of the customary media desire to introduce an element of doubt into a metaphysical concept so as not to risk offence to the sceptics.

It has long been clear to me that whenever there is a discussion or a programme on what, at this point, I will call the paranormal, the sceptics or debunkers as I view them are let loose. Their object being to overcome any real opportunity for the discerning person to weigh up the situation for themselves; operating, as they do, with the delicacy of a sledgehammer approach to quieten their opponents who may well be subjected to ridicule in the process. Verily, the celestial truth seems to burn within the souls of such disbelievers.

Scientists and others, but especially scientists, require and demand evidence-based proof for any hitherto unproven fact or discovery which after exhaustive testing can then be added to the knowledge and store of information and learning for the progress of mankind. That is the way for the physical world, the world of matter, and I will present no argument here. But the ethereal world, which is often beyond that of the physical and everyday senses of most people who are locked into a struggle just to work, eat and survive, is absolutely above the need for proof in the Earth-based scientific requirement.

If sought, nevertheless, the spiritual realm does provide evidence every moment, every hour, every day, every week, every year of our time – always – but is unattainable for scientists and others employing their solely rational minds, concepts and instruments. Fortunately there are some scientists, engineers, doctors and technocrats who do know the all-pervading spiritual world, can access it and link in with non-scientific spiritual workers to help bridge the divide. As an engineer I happily include myself in the former category.

By the end of my journey along the M4 motorway that night, having heard the scientist presenter's remark, it was clear to me that it was time at last to take pen to paper and set down the innate knowledge and learning which I was privileged to possess so that it could be passed on for the benefit of humankind.

2

THE CALL

There must inevitably be a host of reasons why an aspiring author should put pen to paper, ranging perhaps from a desire to seek fame and fortune, maybe an eagerness to tell a life story, one's own or that of another, or the need to convey learning of a nature that might otherwise be denied their fellow beings. While there are undoubtedly many other considerations it is the latter reason why this book is placed before you, and while I could justly claim it is a desire to serve God and to be of spiritual service it is the particular pathway laid before me to attain that goal that can fascinate, culminating with that self reminder on the motorway.

While I have always enjoyed writing and find it a not too difficult accomplishment, I do not easily recall the idea of producing a book as ever being high on my list of things to do. The first nudge for me to think about it was a few years after I started a series of weekly spiritual healing meetings at St Mary-le-Bow church in the City of London ('Oranges and Lemons') under the patronage of the then Rector, the Rev'd Victor Stock, later the Very Rev'd Victor Stock, Dean of Guildford Cathedral. During one of the very well attended meetings of the time a woman engaged me in a positive discussion about my teachings, which regularly took place on a different occasion. Eagerly seeking more information she asked where one might obtain a book on what she had heard from me. Unhesitatingly, I quipped, "I haven't written it yet."

While my remark was meant to be in a humorous vein it nevertheless reflected a truth in that, while some of the learning given her would appear in one or another of many most truly worthy published volumes, none might encompass the mix of information gleaned from me, as with many teachers the way I saw things with maybe privileged information might only be contained in my own teaching portfolio.

Just as in most disciplines and professions where one is advised to have a peer member to consult, I was recommended somewhere around this time by Margaret Sharland, a most experienced medium and spiritual facilitator in whose circle I sat, to seek a meeting in Fulham, London, with clairvoyant Peter McDonnell, a most gifted medium. Acting on this advice I experienced a series of sessions over those years with Peter, and it was on one such session I was advised that our friends in spirit would like me to write a book.

Keeping that request in mind, events moved on until around the turn of this century – the millennium – when certain information came into my possession causing me to dwell and write briefly on the work of the renowned psychic, the late Maurice Barbanell, who had been a sceptic until attending a spiritual meeting during which he underwent an immediate and complete transformation. After that experience he became the working partner on Earth for a high-level teacher in spirit, going on to perform a lifetime of distinguished spiritual service. A fuller account of this event appears in chapter 25, 'Nothing New Under The Sun'.

My regular spiritual healing and teaching work continued unabated after these events, alongside domestic and other responsibilities, until Wednesday, 1st May, 2013, when in the evening of that day Mark Lewis, a fellow healer at the time at the church of St Mary-le-Bow, welcomed me at the Wimbledon Spiritualist Church where he held a pivotal role as a healer. We then had a healing session before moving in to the main church hall. The hall, which was larger than I had expected, had no more than about a dozen people sitting near the front who were being addressed by a clairvoyant medium upon the platform.

We had barely sat down roughly halfway back in the hall when the medium on the stage rapidly turned in our direction and exclaimed joyfully while holding a hand in the air as though clutching something and moving towards me that there was a lady here for me with a red rose in her hand. This gelled with me immediately, being my late wife Jacqueline to whom the red rose had always been a token of affection between us, and these beautiful flowers had been placed on her country grave virtually every week since her interment four years earlier – the practice continuing to this very time.

Just as the medium was finishing this news for me he broke off almost as abruptly as he did when first turning towards me, to proclaim, "Maurice Barbanell is here – you haven't written that book yet." (Remember the name?) For the record, apart from my article years earlier where I mentioned the name, which few if any currently know about, I have not since been in communication with anyone over the matter. As for the medium – also described as a 'sensitive' – I had never knowingly seen or met him before and it took another three years to catch up with him at a venue in South London. He is David Chapman, also of London.

So, now having veritably gone full circle from first hearing I ought write a book, to my experience on the motorway, I am in little doubt that our friends in the world unseen, the Realm of Light, are most actively encouraging me to get down to the job: the task of bringing an understanding of the life eternal into mainstream realisation. The call is heard, hereby acknowledged and answered.

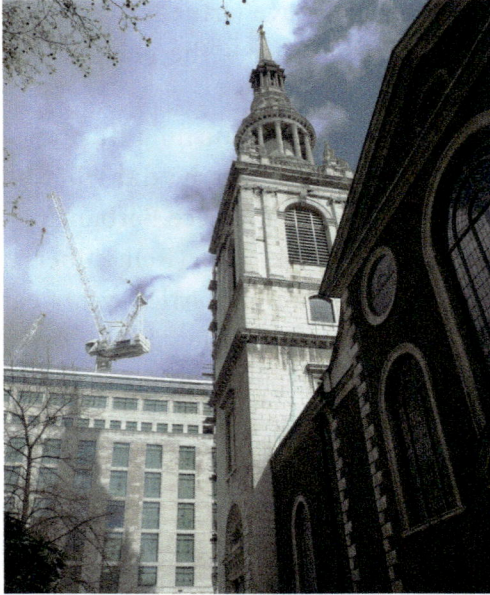

©St Mary-le-Bow archive

ST MARY-LE-BOW CHURCH

A view of the tower and steeple from the Christopher Wren church in the City of London, built 1671-80 and largely preserved during an air raid towards the end of the blitz in May 1941 when the main church was mostly destroyed. Rebuilding took place after the war. The Normans built the first known church on the site in c.1080.

It is from this tower that the famous Bow Bells ring out as they have done for centuries. Legend has it that Dick Whittington from Pauntley in Gloucestershire heard these bells on Highgate Hill when about to leave London in the late 14th century to seek fortune elsewhere, the sound of their peel telling him to go back and try again, from whence he became thrice Lord Mayor of London.

The sound of the bells is embodied in the famous nursery rhyme 'Oranges and Lemons from the line "I DO NOT KNOW SAYS THE GREAT BELL OF BOW".

It is well believed that to be a true London Cockney one needs to be born within the sound of the Bow Bells. This stipulation has, no doubt, reduced the number so qualifying over the years due to noise pollution and the reduction in residential population in what has emerged over time as a world-leading district of finance and commerce – the 'Square Mile'.

3

THE BOTTOM LINE

To come straight to the point we will deal with those questions so frequently asked; What happens when we die? Do we really go to heaven? What is the meaning of life?

The ambiguous answer is that while everybody appears to die nobody really dies and all are eligible for the next world. We will explain this and the reason for being here.

Once having been created by God in His image as you are, life is everlasting – you cannot die. That is the real you, the immortal soul and spirit, journeying through the ages past and/or those to come in any number of lifetimes. Nothing will take that away from you. But we are aware, of course, that whatever other part of us may have everlasting life our body will not survive beyond its allotted span of time in each incarnation and this is what we know as physical death.

It has to be said here that while the teachings of the Church and various holy institutions are prepared to accept a belief in life after death there is a reluctance to embrace the philosophy of reincarnation – a succession of lives throughout time – accepting only the principle of resurrection after death in the present lifetime only, and then under certain conditions. A reason for this, which has led to a conditioning of minds over the years, is explained later.

So, if the expired physical body is laid to rest after its decease on Earth what happens to the everlasting and real self? Answer: it passes into the World of Spirit, also called Heaven, to some the Realm of Light and to others Nirvana, all of which encompass the material world and the environs where we dwell but on totally different wavelengths and, therefore, unseen. The nature of the passage from the earthly life is dependent on the kind of existence hitherto led and the beliefs of those passing over.

We now come to the last of the three questions raised: the meaning of life.

Taking into account what is said above, we – that is our soul/spirit – having been created by God are eternal, and having once commenced our long journey through time and space are seeking ultimately to return to God, its source and creator. This can come about after having acquired a goodly measure of earthly and heavenly learning experience to develop its spiritual growth and evolve to a level where it can enrich the Godhead with the purest and finest of collective intelligence.

These are the answers in short to these vital questions, more of which will now be laid out in detail in the following pages under various chapter headings, together with supporting information, to give as wide a picture as possible of all that comes together to define life on Earth and in Heaven.

In a similar manner to past teaching courses the matters discussed in their order of presentation may be found to be included in more than one chapter as the subject matter as a whole is progressively drawn together.

To provide as broad an understanding as possible of the supreme and universal authority of the work of God throughout His Kingdom on Earth as well as in Heaven the following two chapters first review life in our known and incredible environment.

4

THE COSMOS AND US

Anyone who thinks that tales of the supernatural are a bit far-fetched needs hear of the seemingly bizarre events to which we are all subjected on an everyday basis in our physical environment, events which scientists have little problem in validating. So, this is a prelude to help bring an element of balance into the grand order of things.

Let's start with the easy ones, those we really know about when we stop to think but have little or no time to consider as we go about our daily lives.

You are walking along a road in the northern hemisphere, the road is flat and long receding into the distance. Nearby is a railway line which does much the same, and being close to the sea you catch sight of a ship doing likewise. To complete the picture a plane flies high overhead in a completely straight trajectory.

A simple straightforward scene; what's wrong with that? Nothing to begin with, until you think how your cousins in the southern hemisphere might be doing precisely the same as you at that moment but because Planet Earth is a sphere, a globe, they must surely be walking, standing or sitting upside down from you. You know of course this isn't so, but why?

Well, we realise it's our old friend 'gravity', the magnetic pull towards the centre of the Earth, which allows us all to stand upright wherever we are on the face of the planet.

Now, into this scenario we must bring an aspect of reality. We are aware that the road we were walking upon and the trains, ships and planes just can't be going on forever, straight into the far distance, because the planet is round – spherical – approx. 12,750km (7,900 miles) diameter – 40,035km (24,822 miles) circumference, so is it a mirage we see, do we deceive ourselves? It's worth a thought as we go comfortably or otherwise about our way while living out our lives in our own small corners and being either oblivious or not caring about the wonders amounting almost to fantasies placed before us by God in His unbelievably incredible planet upon which we find a home.

Having thought about the situation in latitudes north and south of the equator, let's stop to think of those dwelling on or near the equator itself. The distance around the equator from start to finish, the circumference as given above, is around 40,035km (24,822 miles.) The planet turns fully around on its axis every 24 hours, so we must deduce that those on the equator are being whirled around, like being on a ride in a fairground, at a speed of 1,668km/per hour (1,034mph). How do they manage without being flung off by centrifugal force? Of course, it's our old friend gravity again – that same force we complain about when falling down the stairs or off a ladder. It may be just as well, after all, that nature offers such a hand.

The gyratory velocity will diminish as we move north or south away from the equator, until reaching the poles where it is almost non existent. So every latitude is subjected to it to a lesser extent. If one is standing or sitting at one of the poles it will take 24 hours to turn a full 360 degrees in the tiniest of circles, which is imperceptible.

Continuing with our reflections on aspects of the material world phenomena we turn now to the annual journey of Planet Earth around the solar system, centred upon the Sun which, in very round figures, is 150,000,000km (93,000,000 miles) distant. The orbit is elliptical rather than circular and Earth's speed of travel on its course is reckoned to be about 108,000km/hr (67,000mph). So, for the moment we may say that at all times while the globe is spinning on its axis at supersonic speed, depending where one is located, it is also hurtling around the Sun – at an astronomical rate! Small wonder we don't all suffer from vertigo.

But we are not finished yet. Less generally well known, or subscribed to, is that the solar system as a whole is also orbiting around our galaxy, the Milky Way, over a period of around 230 million years, turning as it goes in cycles of 26,000 years each time, reminiscent of waltzing while revolving around a ballroom floor. Such knowledge lends itself to an understanding of why Planet Earth is quoted as dwelling in the various houses of the zodiac over lengths of time. During the course of a complete cycle of 26,000 years our planet will have passed through the twelve houses of the astrological chart, representing over 2,000 years of passage through each sign.

It is generally accepted in circles of spiritual teaching, and even now by sections of the public, that having recently passed through Pisces we are now in the age of Aquarius, where the planet will remain for about another 2,000 years. The transition has been going on for a number of years of our time and may not be quite complete yet, which is understandable when considering the age of the journey. It is more likely to be a gradual approach, rather than being in Pisces one day and suddenly Aquarius the next. The unrest on the planet has been ascribed for some while to this change, which some would have is already complete – the 2012 concept.

As we progress through this chapter in order to demonstrate the incredible aspects of God's creation which we are ready to accept without disbelief, we can illustrate more and more phenomena we are willing to accept, simply because they have all been validated by science.

To complete this section we just want to touch on the part our planet, and we, play in the breathless enormity of the cosmos. Ours is one planet in a defined solar system in which the Sun, a star, shines along with up to 400 billion stars or more in our galaxy – the Milky Way. Stars have their planets, too, so we have a mind-boggling array of heavenly bodies to view in the night sky. And then we have our close neighbours (in terms of light years,) because nearby is the

Andromeda galaxy, which with ours and other galaxies forms our universe; and then, there are other universes as well, all reckoned to be expanding. Why doubt there's other life in the cosmos?

Where did it ever begin – yes, we've heard about the Big Bang, but what came before that; when ever could one produce something from nothing? God's hand is surely at work.

It might not be thought unreasonable if, hitherto, one imagined Planet Earth to be the hub of the universe, not in the manner of the medieval mind which took the view that the Sun and the stars together with everything else circled around us, but in the sense that life on Earth stood alone in the infinity of the cosmos.

Such thinking is not entirely without merit because, as we will touch upon later, Planet Earth has been devised by our heavenly Father as one of a special nature permitting individual thought and freewill for all who dwell upon it, unless running foul, of course, from the unacceptable behaviour of fellow inhabitants.

This does not, however, preclude the existence of life on other planets throughout the cosmos which may operate in a more collective manner than we can possibly understand and not be able to benefit, therefore, from the freedom of personal choice granted us. There is also no reason for us to anticipate that our counterparts in a far distant life will necessarily appear in the image of the human species, but may well be created in other forms emanating from different origins – what we would unhesitatingly term 'alien'.

After giving thought to the almost incomprehensibility of the universe and all it encompasses it is opportune now to turn our attention to the unbelievably astonishing make-up and working of the human body, which can so easily be taken for granted while it accompanies us on our journey through the rigours of life.

It is also to be realised as a marvel of God's creation in that we, too, are travellers in time and space and not isolated beings eking out a living in a void of absolute infinity.

Each part of the human self working together in harmony – the heart and all organs, blood vessels, cells, senses, glands, the incredible brain and nervous system, and more – not to overlook the abstract qualities of mind and soul/spirit – all are the divine gifts of God enabling us to function as best we can during the daily struggle. Are we not cosmic ourselves?

Attempts are made to demonstrate in fiction and real life that humans are capable of replication in part or whole, whether of living tissue, robotic beings or artificial intelligence. Here the supremacy of our maker stands absolute. Nothing in the way of reproduction could be considered without the existence of ourselves who form the original model. God is paramount; others may follow, which is the most that is likely to happen. Divine authority and guidance will always come first.

But we need to remember that we are not the only living beings on the planet. Among the many who accompany us we might want to think of the primates, the ape family, from whom we are developed, and the many sentient souls who are part of the Kingdom of God – but this is for the next related chapter – 'Historical, Evolutionary & Spiritual Perspectives' – and in part the later chapter, 27, 'Unconditional Love'.

We have now come to our conclusion in this chapter, the point we set out to establish in order to complement later understanding. The worlds we inhabit, both seen and unseen, physical and spiritual, are unified and indivisible – all are part of God's creation. It is simply that we and the material world in which we dwell during our present lifetime are composed of matter and are consequently at the lower rung of the celestial ladder. But that not need inhibit our spiritual pathway.

FOOTNOTE

Calculations and data appearing in this book are based on generally accepted standards of information and are offered for illustration purposes to aid explanation and understanding.

Picture courtesy of BBC's 'Sky at Night' magazine.

STARRY NIGHT SKY

A night sky picture of the star cluster Pleiades in the constellation of Taurus. It is conceivable that Pleiades has had a pronounced effect on the evolution and life of the human race, similar to that of the star Sirius. The name of Pleiades appears in the Bible in Job 9:9, along with the names of Arcturus and Orion. The same heavenly bodies are mentioned again in Job 38:31–32; the constellation Orion also appears in Amos 5:8.

When gazing at the majesty and magnificence of the heavens can one really ever deny the existence of a guiding hand, God omnipotent and omnipresent? Among a countless number of other planets ranged alongside billions of other suns, heavenly stars like our Sun, can anyone really accept that there can be no other sentient life in space?

Science tells us how everything out there, including Planet Earth, is formed from interstellar dust which coalesced after the Big Bang. But who was there before the Big Bang to get things going? That is the big question for some.

Until the mid part of the last century it was not uncommon to be able to look skyward at night and view the beauty of the heavens, even in capital cities; increasing light pollution from Earth since then renders this an increasingly difficult operation.

5

HISTORICAL, EVOLUTIONARY & SPIRITUAL PERSPECTIVES

I n the foregoing chapter we focussed on the almost incomprehensible wonders of the universe in which we dwell. We now turn to the equally astonishing story of the progress of Planet Earth itself in its journey through the ages.

Before so doing it is appropriate to clear the air as much as possible over the term 'evolution' when referring to the development of humankind in our world. The subject so easily lends itself to dissension between those who support the Creationist theory and others who insist that Darwin got it right; the difference between supernatural creation and that of matter – the physical. It is not our intention to enter into controversy but to explain the circumstances as understood by us so that readers might judge for themselves.

We start with part of a simple prayer:

All things come from God and all things unto God must be returned

At this junction it is equally appropriate to mention that there are some persons who will, or might, want to go along with what we have to say but rather than refer to God as the 'Divine Source of All' prefer to employ terms like 'Universal Consciousness', 'Infinite Intelligence', and so forth. Such advocates are welcomed on board as we are aware that God, omnipotent and omnipresent, answers to all such titles and similar which refer to the Supreme Being with due reverence and respect.

We now embark on what is a very long journey, from the very beginning of time as we know it, then through the ages until arriving at the present. Covering, altogether, a period of 13.86 billion years, which is the reputed age of our universe from its moment of creation – the Big Bang.

Fortunately for the sake of our story we can leap ahead by 9.3 billion years until a time 4.56 billion years ago when Planet Earth was formed within the universe as part of our solar system. These numbers, not unlike the cosmic figures in the previous chapter, are truly astronomical. As a more realisable figure, Earth is now 4,560 million years old. Four thousand, five hundred and sixty million, as one would write on a cheque. Just the odd sixty million is surely beyond human comprehension, infinitely more than the mind can really take in when we accept the fact that we were cave men and women less than sixty thousand years ago, just a one-thousandth part of that odd 60m year period.

So, what has been happening over this vast, otherwise unaccountable, period of time? Well, we are informed that evidence of primitive organisms has been found dating from about one billion years after the Earth's formation, i.e. 3.5 billion years ago, then nothing until around the time of the dinosaurs 120 million years ago; over 3bn years of seemingly nothing in between. Dinosaurs lasted some 55m years before disappearing altogether, due, it is suggested, to a comet crash around 65m years ago, although such incident is sometimes disputed.

A step nearer our time comes from the finding of a thighbone reckoned to be six million years old from 'Millennium Man' discovered in 2000 AD; the oldest find until then being 4.5 million years and ahead in its antiquity from the famous find of 'Lucy', being around three million years old. The period between the Earth's formation and now is of such breathtaking length over aeons of time that the inability of the human mind to grasp the significance of development is well understandable, with billions of years giving way to thousands of millions and so on right down to our time.

Efforts are customarily made to produce graphical illustrations of happenings along the evolutionary timescale from when the world was created until now, a task not made easy when realised that almost everything known to have happened has been during the past 12,000 years at the very most; the facts, otherwise, tending to come from archaeology. Our diagram which follows is based on a straight line journey of 4,560 million years, enlarged in detail at the very end to give meaning to 'our time'.

There is little or no doubt that humankind has evolved through the line of the ape family from true apes to Homo sapiens, well within that odd 60 million year period mentioned earlier. The diagram is an aid to the understanding that almost anything we really know about our present civilisation has taken place as recently as during the last 12,000 years. If we extended that period to 100,000 years, or more, as also indicated on the diagram, we would doubtlessly find our human forebears beginning to move around the planet after emerging from their African cradle of civilisation. Access to cooler latitudes would be more recent, especially following the end of the last ice age, around 12,000 years ago.

Evolution of primates – the ape family – progressed through the ages, as did other species of the animal kingdom, until a time arrived when unlike the other species a separation took place between those who would continue in animal form and those who would develop into human beings. And this is where the controversy starts between the schools of evolution and creation.

To begin with, we resort to our little prayer: 'All things come from God'. From the very beginning of microbiological or animal life in any form it has always been the hand of God at work – no other way. Then we arrive at the crossroads when human beings finally evolved from the line of the apes. How? Various suggestions exist but, simply put, range from either a natural continuation of the physical evolutionary pathway (Darwin) or from intervention by planetary visitors or emergence of angelic beings into physical form as a result of a fall from grace, but always the work of God.

And here we come to the crunch point of our discussion. If God can manifest such wondrous physical doings acceptable to our five senses – including, presumably, those of the members of the scientific establishment – as touched upon in these opening chapters –what else might He be capable of achieving beyond regular everyday understanding.

Suggestions that humankind developed in a direct line from our animal ancestry are completely unacceptable; we are the only species that has been endowed with intelligence, a refurbishment of the physical body and a range of emotions, along with other qualities not found in the animal world. This is the work of God, no matter what agency was at work on His behalf, all being part of the divine plan.

Different times for the arrival of the first humans are offered, a likely period being around 35,000 to 40,000 years ago when Neanderthal man was disappearing and the population of Homo sapiens was comparatively low. Renowned researchers in the field of human evolution appear to recognise the difficulty in establishing the time in which the first humans emerged, it being a controversial issue now just as in the past.

Such process could have started in the Stone Age until developing more fully as mankind gave up being a hunter-gatherer some 12,000 years ago to begin tilling the soil and producing his own wheat after the end of the last ice age.

It has been our intention so far to demonstrate that the incredible planet we inhabit and the universe around us are both part of the same thing – God's Eternal Kingdom, from where we originate and to which we return – the Spiritual Realm.

Whether the recorded, known or believed history of the world we know is 10,000, 12,000, 100,000 or even one million years old, the period is minuscule when set against 4.56 billion years of its total existence. This fact might leave one to speculate whether our own current civilisation is all that the world has ever known, especially when one considers the exceptionally long periods between identified or suspected events on the historical chart running, sometimes, into tens of millions of years. Information coming from the higher realms tells of two known previous civilisations and maybe more.

It is seriously suggested that had the dinosaurs not been eliminated, some 65 million years ago, for whatever the reason, humankind might just as readily have evolved out of the reptilian species instead of the primates. Why not? It's worth a thought.

In a talk given on another subject but touching on humankind's comparatively short history and consequent limited development, the following was included:

"If one is to believe or accept that beings from other civilisations in space (aliens) are watching our planet from spacecraft (UFOs) it is because their knowledge of mathematics and science is light years ahead of ours. What is impossible for humankind now is not impossible for them. It is not that mankind is necessarily inferior but just that we have not been at it long enough. For example, if one hour of the clock face, 60 minutes, is employed to represent progress over the last two thousand years, the period of time since the first powered flight took off in 1903 and now leaves little more than three minutes before the hour expires. So we have a long way to go." (See later diagram)

Following on from that statement, we are able to suggest that evidence of a close working relationship between the heavenly pastures, the cosmos and Gaia (Planet Earth) can be witnessed in the ancient study of sacred geometry, invoking, as it does, a knowledge of spiritual grid lines, ley lines, portals (doorways to the heavens above the Earth) and more, not all fully understood yet on the Earth plane, or admitted to be known by the authorities.

The existence of ley lines was first brought to our notice in the 1920s by Alfred Watkins, after which grid patterns of similar energy lines were established throughout the world.

The wider subject has a measure of mystery about it at this time and there is belief in some quarters that portals in space above the planet may provide passage for alien craft (UFOs) to enter and leave our atmosphere. This may be held by some to be in the nature of sci-fi speculation but there is, unquestionably, a lot out there, in a mix of the physical, cosmic and spiritual, for which answers are yet to be found and accepted by our comparatively young and early developed civilisation.

So, again, to help in our understanding of the

indivisibility between the life we know and the greater world beyond there becomes a need to emphasise the comparative infancy of the present civilisation. Earth grids, ley lines, avenues of communication consisting of lines of high spiritual energy throughout the planet, these are unquestionably prehistoric, yet their existence has been generally known for little more than 100 years. Incoming interplanetary cosmic accessibility awaits discovery. A fledgling culture, do we not walk upon the same ground as civilisations long past?

A well known ley line is that known as the St Michael Line, which starts close to St Michael's Mount off the end of Cornwall, not too far from Land's End, then proceeds through South West and South East England before leaving the country in East Anglia for the North Sea. Notable places of high spiritual energy on its pathway include Glastonbury with its Tor, the ancient Avebury Stone Circle, Silbury's ancient mound, West Kennet Long Barrow, The Sanctuary and Bury St Edmunds.

The St Michael Line is typical of similar spiritual and earth energy lines crossing and criss-crossing Britain and the entire planet, points of intersection yielding especially high energies.

Crop circles, these being patterns and designs produced by unknown hands in fields of growing cereal and similar plant life, have also been active during recent years, especially in South West England. These may well be ascribed to the work of paranormal forces, aliens or human hands. It is likely that forces beyond this world were first responsible, only to be emulated later by pranksters who cannot accept the existence of anything happening beyond the limitations placed upon their own five senses.

The following simple one-line diagram is offered in order to help illustrate the enormous amount of time elapsed since the creation of our world, Planet Earth. What do we really know might truly have happened in those 4,500 million years, and more, before our period came into existence? Were there civilisations before that of our present one, which is minuscule on the timescale, and, if so, how many?

Are we descended in whole or part from angelic beings held fast in matter and slowly finding their way back? Have interplanetary visitors been here in those times and have they helped to seed the human race? Could the human race have come from seeding brought in by asteroids and comets? Not forgetting, of course, that our 'physical' background is attributed to that of Homo sapiens. Whatever it may be, it is the hand of God at work.

The linear concept of passing time is a useful method to adopt here as it helps to remind us that chronological time in linear form is a means adopted by man to give relevance and order to life on Earth and in this sense does not exist in the life beyond. There is a great deal to think about far beyond that of our everyday existence, which might well be considered illusory in the wider, grander, greater order of things.

The reputed age of our planet is that of 4.56 billion years (4,560 million) since its creation well after the Big Bang. If we were to take a car journey along a road over a distance of a similar figure, 4,560km, so that each kilometre represented one million years, we would need to be travelling the entire distance to almost the end of the road before coming anywhere near 'our time'.

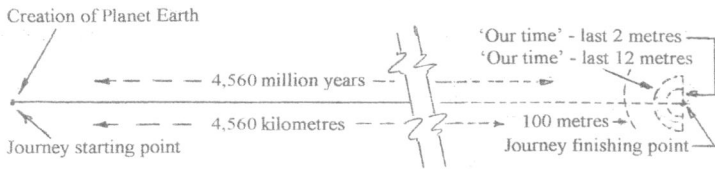

The object of this single line is to remind us graphically that nothing we truly know historically and for which there is direct knowledge and recorded information will be evident until the car in which we are journeying enters the area shown beyond the dotted arc at the right-hand end of the line where it is opened up for clarification. Here it approaches the finishing line with a distance of just 100 metres to complete, equal to 100,000 years, about eight times the span of our present civilisation – 'our time'.

Moving closer still to the finishing line we can reach a final stretch of road 12 metres in length, representing the whole of the past 12,000 years, 'our time'. Going on further we arrive at the very last two metres, the past 2,000 years – now very much 'our time'. So, after a journey of 4,560 million kilometres almost everything we know about our recorded past becomes available in the last few metres.

It's a bit like running a 26-mile marathon. From the start you'll be passing through unfamiliar territory, maybe wilderness and nothing else you can recognise for the whole of the 26 miles, until passing over the finishing line and breasting the tape. Only here at this last moment, somewhere within the narrow width of the line or the tape, will you find the world and the life you have come to know.

So, the past 12,000 years, which equates to our civilisation, 'our time', as represented by the last 12 metres of our 4,560 million kilometre (4,560 million years) journey, is shown immediately below. This is followed by the hour clock diagram to illustrate the very last 2,000 years – the final two metres on our incredibly long terrestrial journey. Indications of times and periods of historic episodes are offered to give perspective.

OUR TIME

The past 12,000 years. Last 12 metres of our 4,560km journey
(4,560 million years)

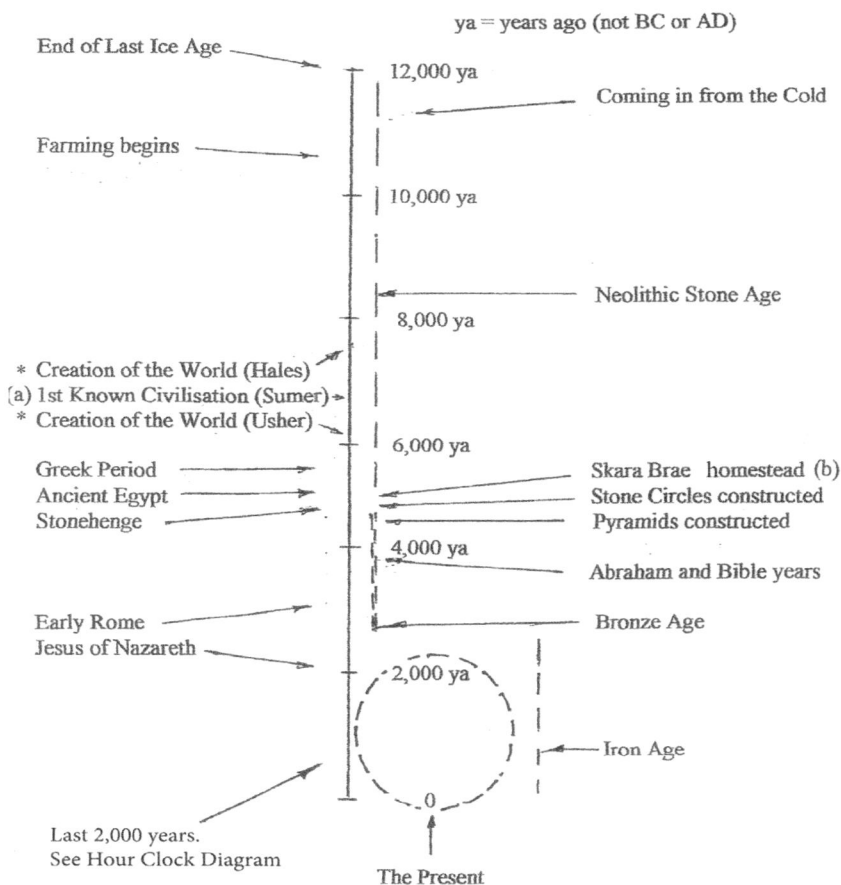

ya = years ago (not BC or AD)

End of Last Ice Age

12,000 ya

Coming in from the Cold

Farming begins

10,000 ya

Neolithic Stone Age

8,000 ya

* Creation of the World (Hales)
(a) 1st Known Civilisation (Sumer)
* Creation of the World (Usher)

6,000 ya

Greek Period
Ancient Egypt
Stonehenge

Skara Brae homestead (b)
Stone Circles constructed
Pyramids constructed

4,000 ya

Abraham and Bible years

Early Rome
Jesus of Nazareth

Bronze Age

2,000 ya

Iron Age

0

Last 2,000 years.
See Hour Clock Diagram

The Present

*For information on Usher and Hales see chapter 21, The Holy Bible.
(a) Sumer: Writing and Law started here in area of present day Iraq
(b) Skara Brae: Preserved Neolithic domestic dwelling on Orkney

What follows is an hour clock for the last 2,000 years showing the minutes ticking away right up to the present time (2018 AD,) since beginning during the time of Jesus (18 AD). This final diagram is intended to illustrate how much knowledge and experience of 'our time' have been acquired in just the most of recent years: science and technology, music and the arts, having been developed only minutes away on the comparative scale.

If 60 minutes = 2,000 years, then one minute = 33.3 years

Left-hand side: 0 minutes to 30 minutes (ago)
- (a) The present time (2018 AD: 0 mins)
- (b) Moon landing (1.4 mins)
- (c) WWll ends (2.2 mins)
- (d) WWl ends (3.0 mins)
- (e) First powered flight (3.4 mins)
- (f) Industrial revolution (7.7/5.3 mins)
- (g) Australia discovered (7.4 mins)
- (h) King James Bible (12.2 mins)
- (j) America discovered (15.8 mins)
- (k) Middle Ages (30.5/15.5 mins)
- (I) Norman Conquest of Britain (28.6 mins)

Right-hand side: 30 minutes to 60 minutes (ago)
- (m) Edward the Confessor (31.3 mins)
- (n) Vikings in Britain (36.8/34.3 mins)
- (p) The Dark Ages (45.5/30.5 mins)
- (q) Romans in Britain (59.3/48.3 mins)
- (r) In the time of Jesus of Nazareth (18 AD: 60 mins)

A very good concept of a similar nature to all that is given above, but on an illustrated timescale basis, is that using the twelve months of the year, counting down from January to December, showing all that happens in what we are calling 'our time' to take place only within the last minutes and seconds of 31st December, the year end!

Emphasis on the term 'our time' used here may be understood when it is realised that researchers of ancient finds might well want to exclaim 'eureka' if evidence of former human life is discovered having an age anywhere near 10,000 years at the most. We are not talking, of course, about finds of prehistoric skeletal remains and fossils, etc.

Absurd, perhaps fantastic, as it may seem, this information is offered to remind us of how insignificant in terms of age and longevity of existence is that of our present civilisation, how young it is when set against the backdrop of the life of the planet, just 12,000 years at the most in over 4.5 billion years. So there must surely be a deeply fundamental and compelling reason for us to be dwelling here and eking out a living on the face of the earth; if there isn't, then why be here at all?

Yet, how many of us going about our daily rounds stop to think and maybe ask ourselves a question: what is this life really all about? Is it really a matter of being born, to live and to die, followed by oblivion? Of course not! That is why these early chapters are focussed on the incredible wonders of the world and the heavens around us which, let's face it, are taken for granted because we know they are there, have always been and, possibly, assume they always will be. But surely there must be something, an underlying reason, a power, responsible for all of this, if we are to make any sense of why we are here!

So, we've arrived at our jumping off spot. We've reached out to seek the unseen hand responsible for this and we've reached God, not necessarily the same deity observed by many to be solely in a highly religious and sacred form but the equally pragmatic God who is there for all who truly seek. This is Spiritual Reality, available for all, which this concise guide will help to demonstrate in the pages that follow.

THE ASCENT OF MAN

This is a straightforward diagram illustrating the evolution of the human species (physical) over the past six or more million years. It needs to be remembered that such a period of time, of lengthy duration to us, is but like a bat of an eyelid when set against the backdrop of the planet's total evolution of 4,560 million years.

Giving thought to the situation, six million years is just a-one tenth part of the odd 60 million years of the total span, so how infinitely small is that six million when considered in relationship to the four and a half billion

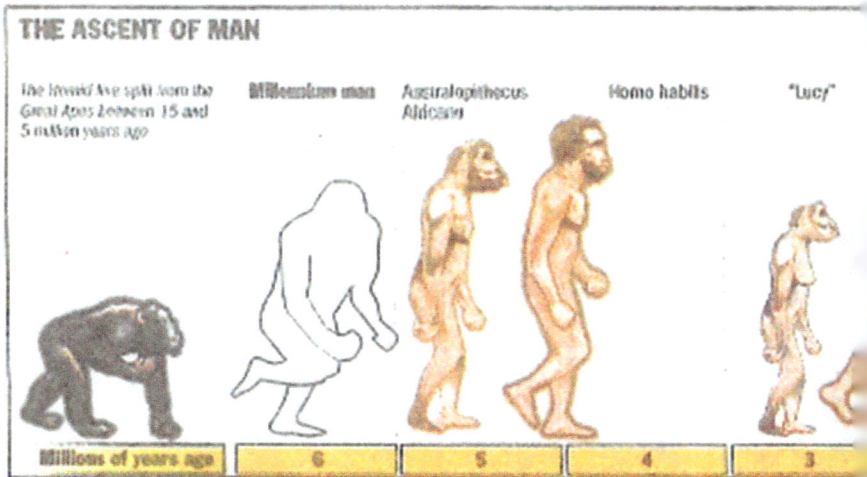

'Daily Express', Tuesday, 5th December 2000

years before the 60 million figure even kicked in? And we must remember that such knowledge as we have of the past six million years is based on archaeological findings, not from known or recorded information – we are without that for even the most part of the last 10 to 12,000 years, otherwise 'our time'.

So, what really happened in those, so far, uncharted years? How many civilisations have there been before ours? How many incarnations might we have had before this present era of little more than 10,000 to 12,000 years?

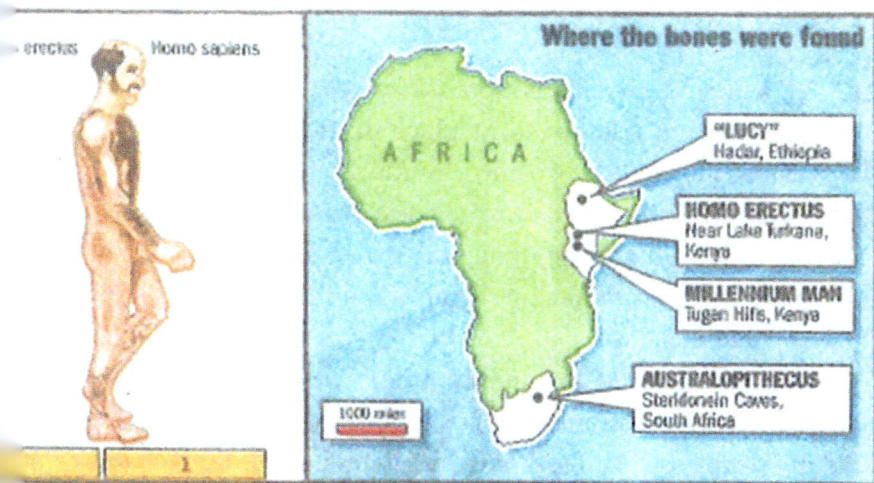

Courtesy of John Lawson/Daily Express/N&S Syndication

6

SPIRITUALITY & REALITY

Having drawn attention to where humankind stands in relation to its place in the grand order of things – the cosmos, our planet, our history and evolution, and planetary time itself – we are now able to concentrate on the fundamental issues which readily prevent so many from having a practical understanding of their spiritual heritage.

What is conjured up in the mind when the term 'spirituality' is mentioned? Piety, goodness, saintliness, religion, devotion? All most worthy expressions and justly conferred on those who are so deserving. But spirituality is for everyone, the good and the bad, the rich man, poor man, beggar man and thief, so the list goes on.

So, the issue here is a matter of degree between what

would appear to be the highly spiritual person and the lesser so. But who is to judge? Only God alone, which in Christianity means the Holy Trinity: Father, Son and Holy Spirit.

Everyone is possessed of a level of spirituality by reason of their inherent and everlasting soul/spirit, and this can be included on a diagram of a family tree where one's parents, grandparents and ancestors show one's personal family background. Running alongside this diagram in a straight vertical descending line can be one's spiritual background – your own personal line of lifetime journeys through the ages.

This means that we are talking, of course, of previous lives – generally known as reincarnation, a word which like one or two others in this area of understanding does not sit comfortably on the lips of many. But that is something we shall be talking about in a while, so just hold on to the idea for the present.

A particular reality of the situation is that no matter how worthy or unworthy you may consider yourself to be, no matter how highborn or lowborn you may feel you are, ALL are EQUAL in the sight of GOD, all treading their pathway at whatever level, and hopefully ever onward and ever upward. Another reality now exposed: life is eternal.

As in many avenues of life one is advised not to make judgement on the spiritual nature and level of development of another. A classic response from a teacher in spirit when asked such a question from a group of students replied: "The man outside the window digging the garden may be more evolved than anyone else in this room."

While there is inevitably a measure of awe alongside

respect and reverence for the mysticism of God and the world beyond, it is our wish that one might now be becoming relaxed and comfortable in the knowledge that we are all part of a great family on both sides of the divide, with little other than a light veil temporarily suspended between us.

A strong aspect of reality now entering into the situation at this point in our deliberations, and one that should provide much assurance to all, is that 'one is never alone'. Each and every one of us has a 'guide' or 'guides' watching over one throughout life on Earth. These may be of angelic nature, or spirits who have had previous physical lives, all being endowed with great wisdom.

It is not uncommon in everyday life to hear people refer to their 'guardian angel' and, perhaps, we use that expression ourselves when a piece of good fortune comes our way. Not necessarily in terms of financial gain but, maybe, when suddenly hearing from an old friend you've been eagerly waiting to connect with, or finding that your very important lost item has mysteriously surfaced. You get the picture. Well, that previously thought nebulous protector is now presented as a real companion in your everyday life. Cherish the idea.

The role of the guide is to keep a watchful eye upon us, to help us steer ourselves through the maze of life: the difficult times and the good times. The situation can be likened to having a reliable and trusted companion by our side, one who does not interfere with our decision-making but who is on hand with a word of advice or a shoulder to lean on when the need arises. This can be felt at times when contemplating a problem, or when asleep or in quiet meditation when we 'go inside' to listen to that 'still inner voice'.

One thing to be certain about is that guides in spirit will not, or should not, attempt to control our lives or tell us what to do. A measure of influence or advice whether or not solicited may find its way to us when we are involved in decision-making. They can help to deter us from entering into and proceeding down the wrong street, literally and metaphorically.

By and large, one has a choice in life to work with the 'Light' or the 'Shadow'. It needs to be realised that the foregoing discussion on the presence of 'guides' about us assumes that one is operating with the 'Light'. The choice or decision to work with the other side, the 'Shadow', must be taken with full regard to any resulting unfavourable consequences. That is why we intimate that those who watch over us with loving care will not be attempting to dominate our lives.

Later on we will be discussing Mediumship and Spiritual Healing, areas where the practitioners are working closely with communicators and guides from the Light. One might ask: "But doesn't God do all this Himself through the Holy Trinity?" Our answer is: of course! But God, with his right and left hand support, is extremely busy. He, they, realise your needs and it should not be beyond our capacity to accept those sent to us in His name; unless, as has been explained, one has decided to back the wrong team.

We proceed now to discuss more cornerstones of the spiritual life, including Energy and Vibrations, The Seven Levels (levels of ascension,) Karma and Soul/Spirit, as well as other important and integral considerations all interspersed with an occasional aspect of science. Earlier we talked about scientists – who have achieved so much progress in taking the world forward with tremendous improvement in the quality of life, when and where properly acted upon – but little realised is that spiritual science precedes physical science. 'As Above, So Below'. Scientific discoveries made on Earth are already known in the world beyond.

7

ENERGY & VIBRATIONS

In a period of less than one hundred years, and increasingly so in the last half century, energy has become a talking point like never before, so it is worthwhile spending a few minutes to consider the implications surrounding this subject from different angles.

In everyday conversation the term might suggest the involvement of personal and physical energy, or perhaps its use in the provision of mechanical and electrical power. If we were to trace the origins on Earth for the sources of these energies we would first need to think of both current and former animal and vegetable life, that is living and decayed, and then acknowledge the Sun, source of all energy and light: God's gift to Planet Earth and all that dwells within. To complete the picture we would then need to think of the air we breathe because without oxygen, which forms just over a fifth of the air in the atmosphere, the combustion of fuel since man first kindled a fire to provide himself with warmth and energy could never have taken place; another gift!

Here we are dealing with physical considerations of energy bearing in mind the all-important spiritual and psychic forms, which are discussed later. For the moment we will continue to ponder on the situation to be found in the physical environment, the world of matter.

The well understood problem is, of course, the unacceptable effect of greenhouse gases and increased temperature in the atmosphere giving rise to the risk of uncontrollable climate conditions due to the burning of fossil fuels. Here we mean the use of solid, liquid and gaseous products such as coal, oil and natural gas, whether for heating or cooling buildings or power for industrial use at all levels; there is also the derived use of oil as aviation, petroleum and diesel fuels in transportation.

The demand for fuel has developed in modern times to a point where its availability and procurement can become an important factor in international relations and economics, and where the locations of such resources can provide nations with almost unlimited wealth. But these resources formed deep down in the planet aeons ago from decaying plant life and animal remains are finite – regardless of proven reserves – which is why alternative and renewable sources need pursuing for the sake of future generations, no matter how far distant.

Energy in all its forms may be thought of as a product of

force, power and movement in varying capacities, strengths and usages depending on the level of the vibrational frequency inherent in the property under consideration. A straightforward example is that of converting ice into steam. Energy from a source of heat can be applied to melt the ice and convert it into water, which will then possess more energy than the original ice, having acquired energy from the heat source. More heat supplied to the water will cause it to boil, and further heat will convert the boiling water into steam, each stage having more energy than the previous as a result of the transfer of energy from the heat source to the ice and then to the boiling water. This process follows the first law of thermodynamics, which tells us that energy is indestructible, capable only of conversion from one state of being to another.

During the process of converting the ice into steam, changes were taking place within the substance due to the increasing frequency of vibration in its molecules as they became more and more excited and agitated by the continuing rise in temperature and, hence, energy content. This now helps bring us to an understanding of how the energy in physical matter mirrors that in the spiritual and psychic worlds, at which we are now arriving, because 'as above, so below'.

Surprisingly for many, perhaps, vibrational energy is one of the most important influences in the structure of the physical world and spiritual life throughout the whole of the cosmos.

We are touching on science now in an area largely neglected by mainstream science where the spiritual aspect is concerned because it would be considered to be not of this world. Paradoxically it could not be more of this world except for the fact it remains unseen to most, being a feature of the soul/spirit as well as ourselves.

The human body vibrates, as does the soul/spirit, which is held captive by the body until Earthly demise when, having a much faster frequency than the physical body, it is liberated for the onward journey. The analogy here being that the higher the vibrations developed, the higher and faster one can soar like a bird.

Everything, everything without exception in the universe, which includes the Earth plane, vibrates at a particular frequency similar to radio waves in the Electromagnetic Spectrum; and here we can refer back to our much earlier concern over the radio science presenter who spoke of a ghost going through a wall.

One only has to visualise oneself sitting in a room within a building having good solid walls all round and then deciding to switch on the radio. What happens? Instant sound! Why? Because the radio waves in the ether have passed through the wall just as if it did not exist. There was no attempt to breach the wall and cause damage but simply to pass through due to the differences in the vibrational frequencies between the radio waves and the wall itself, the latter being fairly low in comparison. And we need not overlook the fact that the radio waves could also pass through our material body, interpenetrating our own vibrations, as is the case, of course, with TV, mobile phones and all similar devices.

Continuing with the radio wave analogy and the science presenter's earlier mentioned remark, the situation with the ghost passing through the wall is no different. The higher vibrational frequency of the earthbound spirit (the more correct title) would have little difficulty in passing through material substances. The opportunity to witness such an event would be vested in those having a level of psychic ability.

We come now to the situation affecting the personal vibrations of the individual, which is paramount in regard to their spiritual development.

During the course of our lifetime, as well as lifetimes beforehand, we are building up a form of credit rating measured in terms of enhanced vibration frequency. That is the sum total of our personal frequency, which accompanies us when we pass over. The higher the frequency, the higher and speedier we consequently go. We are unaware what our personal level of frequency is likely to be, and the act of trying to judge it for ourselves and others will be totally inconsequential.

If asked what one might do to move one's spiritual development along a bit, we would say there are no shortcuts but one can begin to move things along. While continuing to be yourself, start believing, enter into prayer and meditation, accept the reality of everlasting life, lead a goodly life as much as possible – whatever that entails – get involved and be ready to provide service to others in a meaningful way. Handle well the adversities of life as well as the triumphs, either likely being here to try us. Quotations from beyond which speak volumes say: "Service is the Coin of the Spirit" and "Keep On Keeping On".

It is our conjecture that because the holistic bodies (physical and soul/spirit) of sentient beings are vibrating at their own particular level it must follow that some humans with higher frequencies will be equipped with more sensitive natures than others, and some will be higher still. All likely to bring about conditions beyond the comprehension of everyday medical science; as doubtless the reverse can do as well.

Later in the book mention is made of older souls born into the world as Indigo Children, and similar, prepared to help lead this troubled planet forward in due time. Is it not likely that such people, along with others of differing lifestyles and personalities from the considered norm, be of higher frequencies?

For the technically minded and those who would like to know more about this cornerstone of everlasting life, it may be said that the atomic structure of everything is vibrating, though sometimes held in equilibrium. A good example of vibrational frequency in operation is in the oscilloscope seen in hospitals to monitor the heartbeat. The screen will show the familiar sine wave indicating the rate of vibrations.

On a day to day basis one will be familiar with the operation of the electric clock, which in the UK is controlled by an electric current having a frequency of 50 hertz (Hz), the national standard – better understood, perhaps, as cycles per second. A frequency other than this is unsuitable, as it would impair the timekeeping of the clock, as has happened.

Crystals and gemstones which are used as a form of healing (chapter 24) give out energy by reason of the emanations of their vibrations and rays. Quartz crystals, in particular, also have an everyday use in technical processes such as watches and lasers, etc. because of their vibes.

The 'Electromagnetic Spectrum' emanating from the cosmos, as shown in the diagram appearing on page 92, illustrates the wide range of frequencies of wave motion, from long wave/low frequency radio waves to short wave/ high frequency cosmic rays (chapter 15).

An example of the effect of vibrations of a physical nature in everyday life, as distinct from those of the electromagnetic, lies in the ability of sound waves to travel through the air to reach our ears so that we are not denied the ability to engage in the hearing of sound – speech and music. Transmission by radio or telephone where involved can help to a point, but the action of the sound waves passing through the density of the air is essential for the normal process of listening and communication.

The point of interest here is that sound travelling to us through the air is silent while on its way to our ears. The vibrations established when the sound was created will travel silently from the source of their creation until reaching our hearing mechanism, whereupon they will be converted into intelligent words, music or irrelevant sound. This process may be considered to be not so entirely different from radio and telephonic transfer of sound as these produce signals at source which only become meaningful to us as auditory sound when converted by our organs of hearing.

An aspect of energy which one may not so regularly come across is that of Prana, an Eastern term, which like Karma and Chakra, is a Sanskrit word from India (see later).

Prana refers to the life force, the breath of life, which can be explained as the vital energy present within the universe, which can be breathed in by the holistic body including that by way of the Chakra system. A spiritual healer might more understand it as healing energy from the Christ Light.

The breath of life in ecclesiastical terms could well be explained as the Comforter, the power of God watching over mankind during life on Earth and manifesting through Jesus Christ and the Holy Spirit.

The following chapter on the 'Seven Levels' will include further discussion on vibrations; also, any terms mentioned but not fully explained will be covered in their appropriate chapters as the book progresses.

8

SEVEN LEVELS

PLANES OF ASCENSION

By having chosen to read this book it might reasonably be assumed that the reader is either aware or prepared to accept that there is no totality of death to the human being, as regrettably one hears from time to time. Yes, the human body – the vehicle – which has sustained us throughout the present lifetime will drop away, so enabling the soul/spirit which has been captive in our body since birth to proceed to a higher function.

The term 'higher' does not necessarily mean a celestial place far remote in the heavens, but can well indicate an unseen world interpenetrating with our present planet where all worlds co-exist on differing levels separated out by their particular vibrational frequencies, as previously explained.

The soul/spirit does not die. The real 'you' does not die. You are an eternal being. Once created you cannot be destroyed; 'Energy is Indestructible' say the laws of thermodynamics. What remains behind on the Earth plane to be mourned is the deceased physical body, the soul/spirit having departed along with the mental mind, the sum total of your everlasting self through, possibly, many, many lifetimes.

It may be said here that the incredibly wonderful brain stays behind as part of the physical body, it having been an instrument of process responding to and serving the mind. The mind is part of the soul/spirit and goes forward with you, being a treasured aspect of your everlasting self.

Having departed the present life, the soul/spirit is now free to journey into the heavenly pastures known throughout all spiritual life as the 'Light' where the light is truly immense – celestial light.

The course of the journey is dictated by the departed one's level of vibrations, which will be affected at this stage by their previous views of the world beyond, their way of life and whatever belief they have in the existence of life after death. Someone who has rejected such belief, shown complete ignorance or declared indifference to the prospect might find themselves in limbo while, as in confusion, now a soul/spirit, they seek their bearings in an unfamiliar world. At any time there are many souls, described as discarnate entities, otherwise harmless, trapped in this way. Sometimes their presence can be sensed. Help, to move them on, can possibly come from the other side as well as occasional support from specialist helpers on this side of life.

The presence of ghosts is a little different from discarnate entities in that they have usually been around for a long time due, perhaps, to a traumatic experience at the time of passing over or because they remain in a familiar previous life environment in fear of moving on. It is sad that there is an element of people in life on Earth who find fun and pleasure in seeking and pursuing trapped spirits of this kind who really need our prayers, together with whatever help can be provided from workers in this specialist field of understanding.

The suggestion of sceptics that apparitions are the results of events impressed upon the ether must surely be dismissed in the manner deserved.

We return, however, to the customary form of ascent for those departed without having problems in passing over. After release from the lifetime strictures of the physical body, the much higher vibrations of the soul/spirit will enable a swift journey to be made to a place in the Light. It is widely accepted that there are six levels of ascension and one at the Earth level, making Seven Levels in all, each level being sub-divided into seven more levels, and then possibly more, leading to almost infinite grading.

The physical level is the lowest of all the Spiritual Planes and in its higher sub-divided levels also accommodates the Etheric body of man. Then comes the second level – otherwise termed the 'Astral'.

The Astral can be considered as being separated into two principal levels, the Lower Astral being the sphere into which, for example, those having led less desirable lives on Earth will find themselves due to lower frequency of vibrations, while the upper levels are often known as Summerland where most good souls will ascend after leaving the physical.

Summerland can be thought of as a kind of transitional level where one may meet loved ones and friends who have gone over before, even from former lifetimes. It is also where being freed of the density of physical restraint the Spirit may wish to adopt an illusory form of an agreeable lifestyle while awaiting onward movement, or to return to Earth in order to improve its level of spiritual development.

It is in the higher echelons of the Second Level, the Astral, where departing souls from life on Earth will find themselves in a veritable paradise with all the attendant services previously thought to exist only on Earth but there at a far more advanced stage. There are Hospitals for souls arriving from the physical level in need of treatment, such as those having sustained traumatic experiences before or during passing over. There are Halls of Learning to further one's spiritual and general development, and it is to these and other places that one might visit from Earth during the sleep state.

There is reckoned to be the most beautiful floral and colour displays of kinds unknown on Earth. There is wonderful music, too, which one might easily imagine to be the Music of the Spheres, except that this ancient concept is silent and of a mathematical nature more appropriate to the gyrations of our solar system throughout time, as mentioned in chapter 4.

Dreams into which one enters in the sleep state might

be played out here and useful guidance obtained, assuming they are remembered sufficiently well, if at all, upon waking. The elders of Native American tribes would hold dream sessions in the mornings for the overnight dreams of their people to be worked out.

Access to the various levels is dependent upon one's spiritual development, the higher levels being, as one would expect, for the more highly evolved. Those with little or no vibration due to former negative lifestyles will remain at the lowest appropriate level for as long as it takes to respond to a more positive way of being. There is no hurry as there are aeons of time, and remember all are equal, it's just a matter of progress over time; all can get there in the long run.

The third level may be thought as one to which the more highly evolved souls/spirits will ascend, either directly from life on Earth or after a sojourn in the upper second level. This may be thought of as a level for the Mental and Intelligence aspects to flourish as the ascension continues towards the Godhead.

It may be said that it is at the fourth level that spiritual streams of intelligence are beginning to merge with corresponding higher streams on their pathway to infinite intelligence while still retaining their individuality. From this level too, but not exclusively, sensitives on Earth – mediums – are able to receive higher-level communication and learning that is documented or verbally passed on for the benefit and enlightenment of humankind.

The fifth may be seen as that of the highly ascended spirit for whom gradual fusing into the realm of collective intelligence has been, and is, taking place, leading to the sixth and seventh levels; the Hierarchy of Heaven and, above all, the Seat of God.

The concept of levels as customarily used to denote planes of ascension may put one in mind of a typical building construction comprising seven floors in ascending order of spiritual evolution. Another way of viewing the concept is to consider separate spheres representing each level. As with the floor levels idea, each sphere of spiritual evolution will be representative of a higher level of vibrational frequency, proceeding from the first level, the physical, and moving onward to the highest, the seventh.

In reality these levels or planes of ascension do not operate in strict orderly procession but exist independently at their own level of energy, interpenetrating with the levels below their own. In this way it can be seen that the seventh level, the Seat of God, has dominion over all levels, as would be expected. Proceeding with this understanding it is possible to realise that all levels above that of our present one, the lowest – the physical or matter – are readily able to access our space, as happens all the while, though unseen by most.

Having already expressed elsewhere in simple terms one of the laws of thermodynamics, we can now similarly introduce another which tells us that energy can only travel from that of a higher source to one that is lower, and not vice versa. This confirms the meaning behind the above explanation, remembering, too, that – 'as above, so below' – spiritual science precedes that of the physical.

So, it can be demonstrated that a soul/spirit at a higher level, endowed with greater vibrations and energy, can make a visit to a lower level, but none can reach up to a level above their own. Access to higher levels can result from spiritual development while in this world and/or when as a soul/spirit in the 'Light'.

A question often raised on this side of life asks, "Will I meet loved ones who have gone before me when I pass over?" The answer is invariably "yes", and possibly guardian angels and friends in spirit, too, who have long watched over us, and maybe some with whom we have shared previous incarnations. We also tend to belong to soul families, who may also be there to greet us.

FOOTNOTE

It was with agreeable surprise that during a visit many years ago to the holy city of Isfahan, in Persia, a wall-hung painting was located in a room off the main square which appeared to include a theme of the Seven Levels. It was thought that this might have been of Zoroastrian origin, one of the world's early religions, although that could not be verified.

Further reference to the Seven Levels appears in the following chapter, 'Reincarnation'.

9

REINCARNATION

This can be a difficult matter for some to accept, amounting, even, to outright rejection in certain instances: the concept, the reality, of a succession of lives throughout time. This is not due to the subject lacking validity, because it is an integral part of the spiritual existence whether or not one chooses to believe, accept or dismiss the fact. In some members of the public, resistance has been found in the way of their metaphorically closing their eyes and ears, maybe out of fright or simply not wanting to be aware of something beyond their ability to comprehend – fear of the unknown.

In some cases it might be due to the influence of the Church which, it must be assumed, customarily adopts the position that because it was removed from the teachings of the Church some 1,500 years ago, that is how it should remain. This was at a time, of course, when reading and writing was unavailable for ordinary people and the Church hierarchy kept a firm hand over their control.

Reincarnation needs to be regarded as a cornerstone of the life eternal, and its reality will be borne out for all in the long run.

Here, it needs to be recognised that some of the customs and beliefs both within and outside the Church probably owe as much to long established tradition, fear and superstition, as to fact and reality. Tinkering and manipulation with consequent bending of the truth throughout the years to suit intended purposes will have permitted each man-made idea to gain a foothold and acquire an apparent truth of its own and a likelihood of unquestioned acceptance.

Fortunately, where the Church is concerned, we do have enlightened ones to speak out. Among the members of the Anglican Church, ordained and lay, there is a fairly widespread and well supported society – the Churches' Fellowship for Psychical and Spiritual Studies – founded over 60 years ago and having had the Bishop of London as its leading patron; although it is made clear that patrons do not necessarily endorse individual views, neither is there necessarily unanimity of agreement among members.

Around 1969, a canon of the Church, who was a vice chairman of the Fellowship at the time, gave testimony in published form to the belief that reincarnation had been a 500-year-old tradition in the Church until anathematised by the Church in AD 553, as it was then held to be a corrupt form of the teaching of Origen, an early Christian writer. Origen considered that the soul had neither a beginning nor an end. It is not clear whether the belief of reincarnation was ever formally rejected from Church teaching, especially as the council for dealing with the matter was not properly constituted.

Origen lived in a period between the second and third centuries after Christ and was widely respected throughout the holy lands of the time as a most distinguished and learned theologian. It is known and accepted in spiritual circles of advanced thinking that he wrote about reincarnation and upheld such knowledge until it was eradicated from Church teachings in the 6th century at the behest of those who so wanted it expunged from further acceptance, this being the situation which tends to remain in the Church to this day.

He was familiar with the works of Pythagoras and other great esoteric writers who preceded him before the birth of Christ. Pope Benedict has paid tribute to Origen of Alexandria by writing that he truly was a figure crucial to the whole development of Christian thought. (Origen 185-254 AD.) (Pope Benedict XV1, b. 1927: Pontiff, 2005-2013.)

There are those who have given testimony in the present age to the recall of a former life on Earth. A goodly number have achieved this, too, through the process of regression therapy in which they may have had recourse to any number of previous lives. Of these, some might have been in the Church, a monastic order, or high, middle or low ranking in historical settings found in ancient and newly discovered lands, or simply of a more local and domestic nature.

A number or psychic portraits appearing later in chapter 23 are representative of companions in spirit who would have had connection with the author during former lives on Earth – or in Heaven – over a wide range of earth time.

We can now go forward to discuss the part we play in the process of reincarnation.

Having departed this life, the soul/spirit – of those without what we might call complications – will duly arrive in the Light to be met and greeted as previously explained. This may often be at the second level, 'Summerland'. The level ultimately reached will be dependent upon one's spiritual energy in terms of one's frequency of vibrations; the higher, faster, and hence lighter, the higher one goes.

It needs understanding here that the process of going over and levelling out is not in any way in the nature of a competitive race but subject only to the amount of spiritual development built up over any number of former lifetimes as well as the most recent.

The process may be more likened to school days on Earth. One starts from scratch in the lowest class for beginners and step by step makes progress over time until reaching a higher plateau. Just as all are equal in the sight of God, all in this scenario are moving forward at different levels, none of which are deemed to be better than any other, simply at different stages. And there we have a useful comparison, as the older souls at the higher levels, ones who might have experienced countless incarnations, are there to help and guide with their absolute wisdom and infinite spiritual intelligence. At the highest levels this is the 'Hierarchy of Heaven'.

Upon settling after arrival the incoming soul/spirit has a variety of options: there is Hospital if needed, or rest for awhile, or there is learning available, or useful work to be done. Spiritual development can be entered into, or now or later there may be a desire or reason to return to Earth and reincarnate. The reason for this may be as a guiding force for others who are incarnate, or it may be to obtain more experience on the Earth plane to enhance one's own spiritual development. Some may just want to return as soon as possible because of the attraction of the world left behind.

For souls returning to Earth, as in the last instance, another incarnation will assist their spiritual development if they are able to seize the opportunity; if not, the complete lifetime will not be at all progressive and may even finish up being counter-productive, meaning a return to Earth eventually to go through that opportunity again, like re-sitting a failed exam. This may not be such bad news, one has a lifetime of eternity to move forward, but this may be lead to more anguish for one's self and others.

In preparation for a return to Earth when the opportunity presents itself, the soul/spirit working in conjunction with helpers on the other side has an opportunity to select where and with whom they would like to be reborn. This takes place, and the cycle of reincarnation is completed.

As was touched upon earlier, spiritual understanding discussed in one particular chapter may well appear in other areas of explanation; for instance, there is more of reincarnation to follow in the next chapter, 'Karma'. Reincarnation is sometimes known by other names: Transmigration, Recycling or, simply, Past Lives/Other Lives.

10

KARMA

THE LAW OF CAUSE AND EFFECT

This can become a very misunderstood aspect of the spiritual life, even to the extent that on one notable occasion it created a problem in the national life of the UK, finally reaching up to the highest echelons of government.

The starting point for any ambiguity is in the Epistle of St Paul the Apostle to the Galations, chapter six, verses 7 and 8 from the New Testament given here from the King James Version of the Bible:

> 7. Be not deceived; God is not mocked; for whatsoever a man soweth, that he shall also reap.

8. For he that soweth to his flesh shall of the flesh reap corruption; but he that soweth to the Spirit shall of the Spirit reap life everlasting.

Weird and unhelpful interpretations of these verses have led to charges, such as 'sins committed in past lives being the cause of afflictions brought in, or developed, in this life', and consequently viewed as 'Bad Karma' – a form of punishment.

But Karma, from the Eastern traditions, is intended to convey an understanding of a state of being which is neither Bad nor Good but one of Balance, the opportunity to move through any number of lives to enhance one's spiritual evolution and move closer to the Godhead.

A practical example might well offer an appropriate interpretation: a person in their present life has been of criminal intent; passing to the 'other side of life' the soul/ spirit of that person is given every opportunity to reflect on the negative way in which the life was spent so that after a period of rehabilitation there can be a decision to return to Earth and make amends, as this can assist the person in their evolutionary development.

A humble lifestyle can be chosen to reflect the need for improvement. If all goes well that soul/spirit will eventually return to the Light having assuaged a measure of its karmic inbalance, so enabling its state of evolution to move forward. Should that person have failed, however, to live up to their positive intentions on Earth and slipped back into the old ways, or even worse, then that lifetime opportunity will have been nullified and the whole process will need to be repeated again, and again if necessary, until the misdeeds are expunged. There is no hurry; there is millennia and more to climb the ladder. It is a matter of choice governed by the soul/spirit itself in its eternal drive to move forward – even if thwarted.

It has to be remembered that the person in that example would re-enter the world, be reborn, without knowledge of the background described. A question sometimes raised is 'Why do we not remember our past lives?' The answer to that is that a very few do at a psychic level, and some undertake regressive therapy, but the overwhelming majority have no such memory and, possibly, would not want to know if given the opportunity.

Our answer to this situation is what value can be placed on one sitting a scholastic exam on Earth if one had prior access to the list of questions to be asked. Any satisfaction likely to be derived from successfully passing the exam would be of a hollow nature and prove nothing of the individual's worthiness to succeed in life.

On coming to Earth one will meet many challenges and opportunities which might well be denied one if the desired course to take was clearly known. The conditions met and overcome, when necessary, are what helps to mould the character.

Planet Earth is an excellent proving ground for spiritual development – spiritual evolution. A mixture of human types, and many other features, may be more readily available here than in the spiritual world – the Light – where one will be more among souls/spirits of one's own level; though not always, as spirits do undertake special assignments outside of their own environment.

There are many instances on Earth when particularly

heinous crimes leave people wondering if justice will be done or will the perpetrators 'get away with it?' The answer to this question is that nobody 'gets away with it' on the other side even if it appears so on this side. Over there is the 'Akashic', and it is in the 'Akashic Records' that a full inventory of our deeds is kept. The records are in the keeping of the 'Great Lords of Karma' who will ensure that justice is done. The level of justice being, as already pointed out, where the particular soul/spirit now devoid of spiritual energy will spend the equivalent of many lifetimes sorting itself out in the lower plane, until raising itself from the morass by its own efforts and coming to Earth or taking another pathway to try again.

A footnote to the karmic situation is that there is no such thing as failure – only experience. So, if at first one doesn't succeed then try, try and try again. There is an eternity in which to get things right.

There is an aspect of positive Karma where an incoming soul/spirit may take on a particular lifetime in which to be of service to a person already on Earth, or to a certain group of people in a situation requiring special spiritual help. This is a voluntary step taken without thought for oneself and this can lead to enhancement of one's evolution.

Before leaving this chapter it would not be unreasonable to mention that there is a school of thought which suggests by way of interpretation that in the early pages of the Bible there is evidence for the existence of 'Karma'. This is drawn from such passages as those of – 'visiting the iniquity of the fathers upon the children unto the third and fourth generation' – as appearing in Numbers 14:18, also Deuteronomy 5:9, and similar in Exodus 20:5.

This proposal hinges on the understanding of reincarnation whereupon it is suggested that the word 'generation' may be interpreted as 'incarnation'. Meaning that souls/spirits will have to balance their own karmic debts when incarnating in future lives on earth and not have personal indebtedness placed on possibly innocent descendants. A thought-provoking idea granting substance to the understanding!

11

SOUL & SPIRIT

It has probably not gone unnoticed throughout this book so far that any mention of soul and/or spirit has usually been expressed in a conjoined form – soul/spirit. This has not been without reason because it has been leading up to a closer scrutiny of these aspects of our very selves than is normally received.

Both words are in common usage in the English language, but when employed in spiritual or even everyday speech we find they easily become anomalous. In other words, what does soul mean and what does spirit mean?

Dictionaries and books, spiritual or otherwise, as well as the spoken word, quite often tend to mixup the meanings of these two most important words. Here, for example, are some meanings extracted from wider definitions in an English dictionary:

Soul = Spiritual: Spirit = Soul.

And, from a US dictionary, Soul = Spiritual: Spirit = Soul.

In speech we might say 'he, or she, is a 'Good Soul', and be less likely to say a 'Good Spirit'. We may pray for Departed Souls and for Souls at Sea but not for 'Spirits' in such instances. If we were to see an apparition going through a wall as postulated earlier by the science presenter, we would say we've seen a ghost or, more appropriately these days, we have seen a 'Spirit' – not a 'Soul'.

Having, hopefully, made our point, we now propose to use the sometimes confusing terms in the ways more usually adopted. It cannot be said that one is thereby calling a 'spade a spade' but we'll do our best to conform to normal understanding.

While on the subject of ghosts, again, it is opportune to mention that in the time up to about the middle of the 20th century it was quite usual in church services to refer to the Holy Ghost, based on the King James' Bible and the 1662 Book of Common Prayer. After that time, with the growing introduction of new translations of the Bible and the use of the Alternative Services Book, the term Holy Ghost began to decline. Though still very much in use in appropriate settings, it might, nevertheless, appear that the terms 'Holy Spirit' and 'Spirit' more readily conform to present day needs.

So, let's look at what these two most highly significant terms mean in both our life on Earth and in the hereafter.

The soul may be defined as a matrix and a housing, permeating and covering the entire body, physical and sacred, with all its lightly attached subtle bodies and aura. The spirit is that divine and vital spark which animates the soul and gives life to the body and soul. The mind, unlike the brain, is outside of the body physical, and being part of the spiritual make-up remains with the spirit at the time of passing over.

A practical analogous example of soul and spirit could be that of a petrol-driven motorcar brand new and standing on the driveway. It has a perfectly good engine and the fuel tank is filled with petrol. The car is ready to move off but something is missing and it won't start. It lacks that vital spark. Switching on the engine, the sparking plugs fire the mixture of petrol and air in the cylinders and the car comes to life.

We can now proceed to discuss the Subtle Bodies associated with the Physical Body.

12

SUBTLE BODIES
& THE HIGHER SELF

When we look at another person what do we see? A physical human being composed of flesh and blood? A sensitive (medium) looking at the same person might see light and colour all around the body – the aura – which to the experienced eye can provide an indication of the all-round health of the person, physically and spiritually. It can also give an indication of the spiritual evolution of the individual.

A different observer might well just see light concentrating around the head of the person, this being the halo or nimbus. In either case the viewers are witnessing the emanation of spiritual energy possessed by the subject.

They might well be cognisant, too, of the fact that their eyes are trained not on a body with a soul/spirit but are concentrated on a soul/spirit with a body – one's eternal self.

This enables us to understand more clearly that the person under scrutiny is not just a physical being but one of a holistic nature. It does not imply that the soul and spirit are exposed to general view but that the evolved effect of their vibrational energy developed over any number of lifetimes is observable under given circumstances.

What has been put before us here tells us that the reality of what we see, what we think we see – the human body – is illusory, as the material composition of the individual is for this present lifetime only. It is the spiritual and everlasting self of many incarnations that is the real person, containing, as it does, the wisdom and character developed through the ages. The extent of the time ultimately spent on the proving ground of Earth is comparatively short when measured against that spent in the true home – the World of Spirit – the Realm of Light.

Further exploration into the make-up of the body holistic brings us to the concept of 'Subtle Bodies' of which there are various versions, including those of Eastern traditions which, though different, have a similarity of approach to the model we use which is better suited for Western understanding. These 'bodies' are real in the immaterial or abstract sense, are possessed by all and are connected at all times to all other of their levels, including that in the Spiritual Realm from where they came.

Shown like annular rings around a tree, the Subtle Bodies interpenetrate within and around us. These are:

1. Physical body: lowest of the seven levels and having the greatest of density.

2. Etheric body: a replica (double) of the physical, a short distance away from and all around the physical body. It is reputed to still give a measure of feeling in a limb after sustaining a loss. Can be associated with the aura as the outermost shield offering protection from invasive elements of all kinds, negative and cosmic. Survives a while after physical death.

3. Astral body: that in which we travel in the subconscious and unconscious – dreams, etc. Voluntary travel to the Astral plane (Astral travelling) is not recommended, especially without competent and supervised training and assistance. There is the Higher Astral (Summerland) and the lower.

4. Mental body: serves the wonderful organ, the brain, of which it is not a part, and endows humankind with God-given intelligence, to separate us from the animal kingdom; survives earthly death and accompanies the spirit.

5. Intuitive body: connections with right and left-hand sides of brain during life on Earth. Right-hand side: intuitive, creative, feminine, close to nature. Left-hand side: rational, Western style, modern society, commercial, materialistic. A balance between the two sides is desirable – male and female. The intuitive can be associated at this level with the 'Emotional', whose

properties, as with the Mental body, distinguish human evolution from all other species.

6. Soul body: that which accommodates the Spirit and encompasses the body holistic, now and always.

7. Spirit body: gives life to the Soul body and contains all the knowledge, experience and wisdom acquired since inception, some of which can be available to us when we are ready to open up to the opportunity.

A term that one may have come across, or will certainly do so in the time to come, is that of the 'Higher Self'. It is included at this juncture as it tends to encompass the more developed and spiritual aspects of humankind to be found in the subtle bodies.

One might well ask, if there is a Higher Self there must surely be a Lower Self? – Good question!

Reference to the diagram of the Chakras – Energy Centres – in chapter 24, Spiritual Healing, tells us it is at the Heart that we have the Higher Centres Starting. It follows, therefore, that the Throat, Brow (third eye) and Crown Centres lying above the Heart will be higher still, all qualifying for a home in the Higher Self which is that part of our spiritual make-up remaining connected – and providing access – to the world of spirit from where we come and return, even though one might be unaware of this during lifetime on Earth.

It follows, conversely, that the Solar Plexus, Sacral and Base (Root) Centres, in descending order, tend to form what is called the Lower Self, which provides the opportunity for us to remain grounded; meaning keeping our feet literally or metaphorically on the ground during our physical lifetime. Psychic aspects are to be found here, too; e.g. psychometry.

Further reference to the diagram of the Energy Centres will show that the energy of each centre according to its frequency of vibration is increasing all the way up the body from the lowest at the Base to the highest at the Crown, which makes sense.

We may well share this hypothesis with what is witnessed in our daily lives and those around us. Love and compassion will be coming from the heart; good words, thoughts and deeds will be originating from the centres above; while the centres below will be dealing, among other things, with the more practical tasks such as getting on with everyday fears and necessities, as well as the pleasures and desires of life.

13

BIRTH, DEATH
& PASSING OVER

To start at the beginning we first need to ask ourselves a serious question. The population of the world just over 200 years ago was around one billion. Now it is seven billion. Everyone alive on the planet has a soul and a spirit, so from where on earth, or elsewhere, have these additional billions come, allowing for the numbers who are reincarnating and those temporarily or permanently in the Light and the world of Spirit?

Serious thought to this question may cast the mind back to the earlier stages of this book when attention was being focussed on the incredible wonders of total existence which defy all understanding and yet cause us to think that there must surely be a Supreme Being – a Great Overseer – whose hand is at the control.

Most people reading this will likely be older souls who have been reincarnating over time, because they are the ones who have been motivated to pick up this book and look beyond the everyday acceptance of life going on around them. But what of the billions of others; from where have they come?

This brings us to the consideration of older souls and younger souls. As already said, one cannot be judgemental in these matters but it might begin to occur to enlightened minds that those with the more settled dispositions are likely to be the carriers of the ancient wisdom, whether or not they are open yet to the realisation. But we must remember that whatever the extent of past life experience, if any, all are equal in the sight of God, treading their eternal pathway ever onward and, hopefully, ever upward.

Having considered the comparatively low population of Planet Earth in earlier days, there may be good reason to suppose that advanced souls could easily be coming from other parts of the universe, and remember, too, those unaccountable astronomically long periods of inactivity in past millennia, as earlier discussed – what legacy might there be? And there are the angelic beings living out their time in physical form that we touched on earlier.

In mainstream spiritual teaching the great Oversoul is mentioned, from where new souls can be created as divine aspects of God, which is what we all are in the long run. It is from interstellar dust that we come together as matter, and as a thought of God that our bodies are 'quickened'.

Some of us in incarnation cherish our family tree; the farther back, the wider it spreads, the better. Some might prefer not to know too much about their ancestral line, immediate or ancient. Others may spend endless time pursuing their genealogy. Whatever one's situation, few will give attention to an inevitable and vital missing part of any family tree – the spiritual line of descent. This, if it could be shown, would be drawn alongside the line, of known heritage coming down in a straight line, with stops along the way to indicate former lives. This is the real you bringing with you all your evolutionary spiritual development, no matter what the extent, and accompanied with all the hopes inherent in a fresh lifetime on Earth.

Of course, one inherits the family characteristics through the physical line of descent, the breeding, the DNA, the features, but to emphasise – you are unique – you are your own person making your own way through a life eternal; no one can take that away from you; you are moulded in the image of God and His love accompanies you wherever you may be – just hold on to it.

We have already explained that, in consultation with the hierarchy, your soul with accompanying spirit has already decided with whom you are to incarnate, which, for example, might well be with members of a family you had a connection to in a previous lifetime. Mention has been made of the great Oversoul; there are also soul families to which we tend to be attached, and it is from, and to, these families that we come and go – a possibility which gives much hope to those bereaved, in that they might again meet up with loved ones. It is reckoned that soul families incarnate over a similar period of time, which increases the chances for re-unification, if only for a while, as the celestial journey continues.

So far as the birthing process is concerned, spiritually and gynaecologically, it is understood, though sometimes slightly disputed, that a measure of the soul and spirit enter at the moment of conception, when the sperm unites with the egg. The foetus with its spirit connection develops within the womb until full-term delivery. Sometimes, unfortunately, things do not work out so well and the pregnancy terminates. This may be due to physical causes or where the spirit of the unborn child meets with problems and decides to return to the place from whence it came, the result being that without a spirit there is no life. A situation like this can even happen after delivery when the incoming spirit may decide to go back. Needless to say, these situations cause much grief and heartache. In the case of the soul's departure after birth, pathological reasons are usually offered rather than those of a spiritual nature.

At any time our spirit has a connection with the higher realms, the amount of spirit in the infant body being of a very small order as might be expected in its process of earthly development. Further stages of the spirit will access the child and then young adult over successive seven-year periods, these being at ages 7, 14 and 21, until at the age of 28 the spirit is fully established; the point at which the spirit itself connects with the physical body being at the pineal gland located close to the brain. This very important gland has a connection with the pituitary gland, also of importance. In fact the glandular system as a whole is associated with the spiritual nature of the person.

The infant, then child, young person, and eventually

adult, will progress through life until its time on Earth in the present incarnation comes to an end and the soul and spirit will be ready to depart back to the higher realms, as earlier discussed, the final separation from the present life taking place upon the dissolving of a silver cord which connects the soul and spirit to the physical body. The moment of passing over will not take place until this occurs:

> 'Or ever the silver cord be loosed… then shall the dust return to the earth as it was: and the spirit shall return unto God who gave it."
>
> Ecclesiastes 12:6 (pt) and 7

Back in its eternal home after an earthly life, the spirit will dwell in the Light, or in less favourable circumstances, as discussed earlier. Longer term progress into the higher levels allows the individuality to be retained during gradual fusion with the stream of collective intelligence.

A matter arising for discussion from time to time is whether the span of a person's time on earth is predetermined or subject to chance. Is it a matter of destiny, fate, kismet or whatever? Is there an overall guiding hand? Do accidents really happen – was he pushed or did he jump? Is there no such thing as coincidence but 'synchronicity', when influences, forces, converge to bring about a resolution?

How often has one heard the expression, "It's meant to be" when circumstances connect?

Our take on this is that God and all who watch over us in His name have control over all things, but within the boundaries of an individual's allocated span of life there may be circumstances arising which require an earlier return. The reasons may not be apparent at this level but they may well be in the interest of the individual – and not because of an unwelcome and sad situation as will quite possibly be felt by those remaining behind.

This explanation is offered in the knowledge that earthly life is an aspect of the total life, and the one who has gone ahead may, for example, have pressing reasons to be back on the 'other side'.

We are not taking upon ourselves to discuss bereavement, which is a very personal matter best left to those who mourn and grieve, and we feel the information given here and in other parts of this book will afford a measure of comfort and hope at such times.

'To everything there is a season, and a time to every purpose under the heaven. A time to be born, and a time to die; a time to plant, and a time to pluck up that which is planted.' Ecclesiastes 3:1-2

14

THE LIGHT

In previous chapters we've seen an occasional reference to the Light; what light, one way well ask? We're familiar with some everyday phrases like: "Let there be light" and "I've seen the light". We're accustomed to daylight, moonlight, artificial light, even the northern light(s) – the aurora borealis – but to what are we referring beyond these?

Here we are talking about the Celestial Light which like the love of God surpasses all understanding. It is a light of such incandescent brilliance and comforting warmth as rarely experienced in everyday life on Earth. It is the Light of heaven that once witnessed will never be forgotten and is available to all on their ageless journey through space and time.

Isaac Newton experimented with light, and demonstrated with the use of a prism that white light was composed of seven primary colours, and is reputed to have said that "Light is the nearest thing to God".

The Bible contains over 250 references to 'Light'; here are just a few short passages attributed to Jesus:

Ye are the Light of the world. A city that is set on a hill cannot be hid. Matthew 5:14

Let your Light so shine before men, that they may see your good works.

Matthew 5:16

He was a burning and a shining Light.

John 5:35

As long as I am in the world, I am the Light of the world.

John 9:5

I am come a Light into the world, that whosoever believeth in me should not abide in darkness.

John 12:46.

There is a most famous picture, 'The Light of the World', showing Christ standing with a lighted lantern at the entrance to the locked door, meaning the soul/spirit and mind. The picture is the work of the pre-Raphaelite painter, William Holman Hunt (1827-1910). A text below the painting is taken from Revelation 3:20:

'Behold I stand at the door, and knock: If any man
hear my voice, and open the door, I will come in to
him, and will sup with him, and he with me.'

The original of the picture is in the chapel of Keble College,
Oxford. A much viewed copy painted with assistance hangs
in St Paul's Cathedral, London. Another copy by the artist
is in the Manchester City Art Gallery.

The Spirit Realm, which occupies six levels above the
physical, is the home of this scintillating Light to which
one's spirit is able to return quickly and calmly at the time
of passing over, assuming all else is in order. This means
that as long as one's understanding and acceptance of
the life hereafter is of a positive nature, there should be
a straightforward transition into the Light. Those with
low spiritual evolution, development and frequency of
vibration, caused by a negative lifestyle and/or refusal
to accept the existence of the life hereafter, may have
difficulty in acquiring their bearings for a while and exist
as discarnate entities until sorting themselves out.

Once comfortably in the Light, the comings and
goings and ascension to higher levels will be as described
elsewhere.

One hears mention and stories of and from people who
have almost died in this life and have found themselves on
the way to heaven – 'near-death experiences' – NDEs. A
common factor in all their accounts is that of proceeding
along a tunnel and seeing a beautiful warming and
beckoning Light at the end. Some have reached the end
and gone further; others have returned sooner, maybe
upon hearing the voice of a loved one calling them back,

such as for a mother to return for the sake of her children. Many have been overwhelmed with the joy of the beauty, warmth and love in the Light and speak of disappointment in coming back. In other instances the spirit may leave the body and witness proceedings around it when, for example, a surgical operation on the body may be in progress while the patient is anaesthetised. This is known as an 'out of body experience'.

It is worthwhile to reflect on the level of light placed at man's disposal in his daily toil on Earth in order for him to achieve the most satisfactory standard of living possible. Natural lighting directly or indirectly from the Sun has been the mainstay of his illumination throughout time, although the amount available for beneficial use will always vary according to location, climatic conditions, time of year and time of day.

In the dark of the night, as well as on darker days, various means have been employed over time to create forms of lighting capable of making life more bearable, these customarily coming from animal products and plant life as well as from fossil fuels laid down aeons ago.

Nowadays there is hydro-electric, wind and tidal power, nuclear energy and other possible methods, but whatever the means of providing artificial lighting it all derives from the munificent grace of God, who through the basics of solar radiation and primeval earth formation has granted us these blessings which can so easily be looked upon as normal facilities in the modern age.

Candles were the mainstay of artificial lighting for thousands of years, probably as far back as the earliest biblical times and beyond, but not of a kind we now take for granted, which is the product of continuous development since the very first candles provided a measure of illumination for early mankind.

While the use of oil obtained in one form or another might have found occasional use for lighting in earlier times, it was not until around the 18th century that it became more widespread in use, thereafter phasing out towards the end of the 19th century with the introduction of 'town gas' derived from coal in its conversion to coke, gas lighting being gradually replaced thereafter by electric lighting during a period from the late 19th century until the early part of the 20th century, after which it has held supreme. (Town gas also gave way to petroleum distillate gas and then natural gas, for industrial, commercial and domestic use, from around the early 1960s onwards.)

Such progress in lighting refers particularly to townships in developed countries, as remote areas took longer, and there are unquestionably corners of the world where these modern facilities on tap, just like water and sanitation, are still a luxury beyond dreams.

There are people who now remember homes lit by oil or gaslight before electricity became universally available, and it was not unusual in the towns and cities during this period to see street gas lamps attended by the lamplighter on his rounds. Buildings of a more public nature like schools are also remembered for having gas lighting.

Apart from any technical and historical interest this information might provide, it again illustrates what we set out to demonstrate in chapter 5, that our world – the civilisation we know and in which we may feel comfortable – is only just waking up from a long sleep after taking the best part of 4.56 billion years to provide such basic considered necessities as gas and now electric lighting on demand, quite apart from all the incredible benefits to our lifestyle that these forms of energy confer.

So, following that realisation, where better than under this chapter on 'Light' – the incredible 'Celestial Light' – the eventual home for all on the eternal spiritual pathway – can we give full expression to our concern contained in a former newsletter at a time when the planet was preparing to leave the 20th century in readiness for its entry into the new millennium, with all the promise and potential for the dawning that lay before it:

> 'Throughout these 2,000 years Earth has been affected by greed and lust for power, and torn apart by conflict, war and genocide – by all the cruelty, bestiality, barbarism and inhumanity which man can devise – and it continues right up to this time. Who could deny that this present century might not have been the worst in which man – and often Christian man – has inflicted so much hate and destruction upon his neighbour.'

That statement was written in 1999, not so long ago in the annals of the life of mankind, as we like to point out, but even so, has anything much, or at all, changed in this 21st century, and now the Aquarian age? It's up to us – the choice remains!

Before ending our discourse on the 'Light' and all that ensues in its train, a few further words on the universality of the candle should not be overlooked.

As well as helping one to see and find the way in whatever context that might be interpreted, the light from a candle is, and has long been, a symbol of worship, hope, peace, love and remembrance, and so much more for all who find solace in that light. It is likely to be found in most places where the human heart seeks something of an understanding coming from beyond itself.

15

THE ELECTROMAGNETIC SPECTRUM

In chapter 7, 'Energy & Vibrations', there was brief mention of the Electromagnetic Spectrum, which is a useful way to illustrate the range of vibrations coming to the Earth's surface from outer space. The spectrum includes a small section indicating the visible 'Light' which it brings into the world and from which humankind benefits. It therefore is a useful follow-up to the previous chapter on that particular subject.

The spectrum is composed of electric and magnetic energy travelling at the speed of light throughout its entire range, in which there is a continuing reduction in its vibrations from the high frequency end arriving from the cosmos to the low radio wave end. As the frequency of vibrations in cycles/sec (Hz) reduces progressively along its path, there is a corresponding lengthening of its wavelength in metres.

One may well be familiar with the earlier locations of radio stations on air being expressed in metres of wavelengths, to be largely superseded by definitions in kHz (kilohertz), meaning vibrations in 1000s of cycles per second. This being a good example of interchange between the two units, either would lead to the same location, except that advances in broadcasting have left very few stations to be denoted on the wavelength scale.

The Electromagnetic Spectrum: Notional Diagram

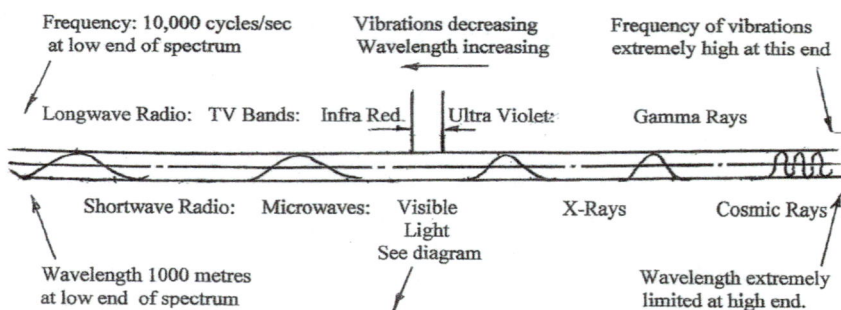

Frequency: 10,000 cycles/sec at low end of spectrum	Vibrations decreasing Wavelength increasing	Frequency of vibrations extremely high at this end

Longwave Radio: TV Bands: Infra Red   Ultra Violet: Gamma Rays

Shortwave Radio: Microwaves: Visible   X-Rays   Cosmic Rays
                                          Light
                                       See diagram

Wavelength 1000 metres
at low end of spectrum

Wavelength extremely
limited at high end.

'Light' as we know it. Enlarged Band of Visible Light (White Light) from Spectrum above

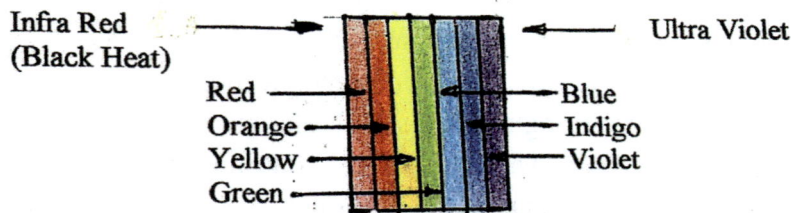

Infra Red
(Black Heat)   Ultra Violet

Red   Blue
Orange   Indigo
Yellow   Violet
Green

Infra red light on the lower energy side of the Spectrum of Light, and ultra violet light on the higher side, are both invisible to the naked eye and should be regarded with caution, from handling dull but otherwise very hot substances to over exposure of sunlight or tanning machines.

The order in which the colours are grouped together is precisely the same as that in the rainbow, being of a natural arrangement, as can also be found by passing a beam of light through a glass prism as mentioned in chapter 14, 'The Light'.

It will be seen from the Band of Visible Light in the Electromagnetic Spectrum above that as the colours in the Light pass from violet to red, from the higher to the lower end, they are progressively reducing in frequency of vibration – hence, energy. The difference may not be that great overall considering the comparatively short length of the spectrum but is sufficient to permit a marked contrast between the energy content in the lower colour red, associated with the base Chakra in spiritual healing, and the higher colour violet at the crown centre, with its strong connections to the spiritual world. See chapter 24, Spiritual Healing, with Chakra diagram.

The seven primary colours which are grouped together to form white light also operate separately as rays of coloured light emanating from the Godhead. This is the situation in cases of spiritual endeavour where, for example, the rays of higher energy and spiritual value like violet and blue can be directed from above to aid soul healing. The healer can be aware of these and other colours received during a healing session, as might the client on occasions.

Not being confined to healing work, the colours may also be witnessed in other forms of spiritual activity, not necessarily from a visual capacity but in the mind's eye.

There are other colours of a secondary nature to be seen in everyday life, as well as those of indescribable beauty not known on Earth to be met in the world beyond.

16

THE ETERNAL PATHWAY

We have been labouring the point that there is only one way to go in the long run – 'Onward and Upward' towards the Godhead. There is no hurry if one wants to take one's time, maybe spending a few more lifetimes on the Earth plane and catching up with some of those opportunities and questionable pleasures missed out in the past. One has all the time in the world – yes, in the world – because there is no horological time there, as we know and measure it here on the linear scale.

Spirit can easily spend an incarnation in the physical life to be followed by the equivalent of an era or more in the spirit world before coming back to Earth to continue the journey. 'A thousand ages in thy sight are like an evening gone,'; a most compelling line from the recognisable hymn:

'O God our help in ages past our hope for years to come'.

The situation can be likened to that of going to sleep and awakening in a darkened room. Unless one has a point of reference at each end, a clock reading before and after, one has no real idea of how long one's been asleep and what is happening now.

The desire, the urge, for the spirit to move forward might be likened to travelling on an escalator between floors in a multi-storey building. Having reached the first upper level, one hesitates and travels back down the other side to where one started. That would be the equivalent of a lifetime. Then one repeats the process, goes up and comes down again, and keeps repeating it over and over again until finally arriving at the top of the first flight and, bracing oneself, places a foot on the first step of the next flight to the level above and goes off. While on the moving staircase one has nothing to do but to hold on – the motion will carry one forward

The forward movement, the inherent desire, to move back to the Godhead from where one was created is like being on a river running out to sea, or as the flight of a homing bird, no matter how long the journey. It is also reminiscent of the action of peristalsis in the alimentary canal where, once food is imbibed, the autonomic system will take over and move the contents forward continuously – an involuntary muscular wave-like motion within the body over which the individual has no control.

Further consideration can be discussed here of the nature of the progress to be made within the Light by those spirits who are really moving forward. We have already given thought to the more usual access into the world of spirit – the afterlife. All being well, entry will first take place in the lower level, Summerland. Given to all souls, however, is their destiny to move higher and higher in the levels, regardless of the time taken. In due time access to the third, and then fourth, levels (also referred to as 'dimensions') will become available to all in their journey to the Godhead. While at these levels and, ultimately, higher, the individuality is retained and there is a gradual merging of the spirit energy into a collective source of finer and purer intelligence.

17

RELIGIOUS
CONSIDERATIONS

W e have been asked on rare occasions, although
the question might linger in some minds,
unasked: "Is your work Christian?" To which
we answer, it is essentially so but that does not mean that
valuable knowledge and beliefs from other traditions or
from our own abandoned past cannot be included.

We should not need to say that there is no denial in
our work of Jesus Christ nor of the Father, Son and Holy
Spirit in the Christian religion. We need to remember
that a great deal of the beliefs and traditions of all faiths
contain an element of man-made customs which have
taken root over the ages, nevertheless a scant amount

of time set against the spiritual evolution of the human species.

Jesus, who was a carpenter, was endowed with the Holy Spirit through John the Baptist in the waters of the River Jordan, thereupon becoming Jesus the Christ. During His preaching and deeds over the following few years Jesus spoke in parables, healed the sick and performed miracles. The Holy Bible contains almost 40 parables, 23 acts of healing both physical and mental disorders, three cases of bringing the dead back to life and ten other miracles. These are all in the New Testament and many appear more than once in the Books of the four Apostles, who went on themselves to perform great humanitarian acts.

Jesus dedicated his life to bringing peace, unconditional love and fellowship to all, yet we feel obliged to draw attention to the bestiality and crimes committed against fellow man over the past 2,000 years, often in the name of The Holy Trinity, and more than enough times by the Church itself. So, do not accept criticism of your belief if you know it comes from the heart and is genuine. As has been said earlier, the testing time will be on the return to the Light when ALL will have the opportunity to reflect on their former life.

In the year of the millennium, 2000 AD, Pope John Paul II, accompanied by key members of his Curia, made a public apology for sins perpetrated against others by the Church, whilst at the same time offering forgiveness for those committed against the Church. (Pope John Paul II, 1920-2005: Pontiff, 1978-2005.)

While we speak here of the Christian religion you are invited to join in our thoughts and words whatever your religion or if you have none at all. Hold on to your truth assuming it to be positive, do not be deterred, and follow the Golden Rule: Love God and your Fellow Man and Woman with all your might for the unquestioned benefit of humanity in which we are all brothers and sisters. There is but one God.

18

THE BELIEF SYSTEM

Coming now to the Belief System, and moving up the scale, we first arrive at Atheism, whose belief is that God does not exist. Full stop. We then come to Agnosticism, which holds the view that nothing is known of God or of anything beyond material understanding. Somewhere around this area we need to let in Humanism, whose concern like the former is for humankind rather than the divine or supernatural. This section tends to cover the Secular, the Temporal.

A number of years ago a man of what would now be termed celebrity standing, and who came across as a strong humanitarian, was asked in a radio broadcast what he thought would happen when he died. "Just six feet of earth" was the surprising nature of the response. That was his view, to which he was entitled having been asked to offer it in public.

We now approach the more spiritually inclined believers, starting with the growing number who hold themselves to be more Spiritual than Religious. This is a worthy position to adopt assuming it means what it suggests, that one pays due deference and homage to God and all who guide from the Light, and is not a reason for backsliding – not bothering.

This is followed up by the Believers, ranging from those who are sincere in their private and personal understanding, up to those who are heavily committed in their faith. Lastly in our abridged round-up we come to those who add knowledge to their faith. They know! Among this closing section might be found those who chart independent courses in the interests of humanity, also the Pentecostal, and the charismatic and latter-day evangelists who have filled the halls and stadiums with great congregations, especially in the second half of the 20th century.

Never to be overlooked are the acceptable, established places of worship, whatever the faith, which work tirelessly on behalf of their congregation. Here in the appropriate circumstances may be found peace and understanding in a welcoming atmosphere.

Synonymous with 'Belief' is that of 'Faith', but is it always? Not necessarily! Devoted churchgoers have been known to question their faith, but that is for them and does not require the judgement of others. Faith can imply that while a person subscribes to a particular religion or cult it does not mean that they accept all the beliefs or even understand the full implications of what that denomination represents.

Terms in current coinage which freely utilise the term 'faith' in its make-up does not suggest anything beyond compliance with a recognised pathway of religious adherence. A form of 'belief' may well not enter into the situation.

To have 'faith', on the other hand, can denote one's absolute belief in God and The Holy Trinity (where Christianity is concerned), going on without any doubt to have unwavering belief in the mysteries of the scriptures and the life everlasting with all that they involve.

Faith in God, in the truth and the afterlife is paramount. Not to be overlooked, however, is faith operating at the human level, especially within oneself. Faith in one's superiors and subordinates, too, is a desirable, if not essential, requirement for the maintenance of good working relations in business, public and everyday life. In the absence of trust, conditions can readily deteriorate to an unacceptable level of operation.

We need to have trust, faith, in those who have our lives in their hands, such as all who care for our health – surgeons and medical practitioners – through to those who transport us around in this age of ubiquitous travel – airline operators, rail, road and sea carriers. Without such trust, modern living could not exist at its present level.

So, if we find it necessary to put our trust quite often in anonymous fellow beings, how much easier should it be to place our trust in God who well knows us and our needs?

Humankind is made in the image of God, it is a part of God. Denying the existence of God is like denying the existence of our parents. If we deny the existence of our parents we do not exist in the flesh. Likewise, if we deny the existence of God, we cannot exist because we are part of God, the part which brings the flesh to life.

One hears that there are those in the world who have a need to claim that certain events in recent history, both epic and unimaginably grotesque, never existed and are products of government propaganda. So, again, we say if God doesn't exist then neither do we exist and we must therefore be an illusion; which, paradoxically, is largely true because it is that part of us unseen by most, the soul/spirit, which is the real self travelling through the ages, adopting the flesh at each halting place. Let the truth resonate.

When seeking one's own answers one may want to question God or those who come in His name, including reassurance over any prevailing doubts. But never, never, attempt to put God to the test; apart from all other considerations, it will be ill advised.

Jesus said…

Thou shalt not tempt the Lord thy God.
                              Matthew 4:7 and Luke 4:12

19

PRAYER & MEDITATION

What is prayer? Prayer means to 'ask'. And that may raise a query. How do we go about it and for what sort of things should we ask?

Occasionally one meets a person who says they very much would like to pray but do not know how it should be done. So this is for them, as well as for general interest. Advice offered when asked is that if you can think, can talk, there is no problem except for overcoming your own stumbling block.

To start with, if one is able to speak to another person or speak on a telephone, then one is well on the way already, because prayer is just like that. Talk to God, to Jesus, to the Holy Spirit but if you are hesitant to approach the Hierarchy in heaven then speak to your guardian angels who are with you, guiding and following you all the time for your own spiritual and earthly well-being.

So, to get going find a quiet place, on your own, then just speak respectfully. You can open your prayer by saying "In the name of God" then tell of the matter in hand which constitutes your prayer. Finish by giving thanks to God, because those to whom you have spoken, have prayed, have come in His name at your request. Give thanks also to your guardian angels and all who have come in the name of God.

If you do not wish to speak to thin air, it is always possible to use a telephone, without dialling, until you become accustomed to the idea. Eventually, if not immediately, your prayers can be offered in silence but that can take its time as long as you begin to open up in whatever way suits you.

Here we are touching on a most important aspect of your spiritual life because the heavenly beings to whom you offer your prayers already know what it is you need to say, but you have to say it – to enunciate your needs. No shortcuts – get on with it!

A most important consideration is to always ask for one's needs and not one's wants. We would not imagine that any readers would be asking for help in achieving personal gain but would be focussing more on personal problems and seeking assistance and blessings for others in difficult circumstances. This is the process of intercessions – interceding on behalf of others; everyone can do it.

A useful reminder: be careful what you wish for – the result might not always be for what you were hoping. Whether or not one prays, always seek to live in the Light.

Drawing negative energy toward you, no matter what the promise, will prove to be most unwise and uncomfortable in the long run, if not straight away.

> 'But thou, when thou prayest, enter into thy closet, and when thou hast shut thy door, pray to thy Father which is in secret; and thy Father which seeth in secret shall reward you openly.'
>
> Matthew 6:6

This passage leads on to the Lord's Prayer, a copy of which is at the end of this book.

> 'Ask, and it shall be given you; seek, and ye shall find; knock, and it shall be opened unto you.'
>
> Matthew 7:7 and Luke 11:9

Meditation might well be described as a close cousin of prayer, but as in family relations there can be noticeable differences. In prayer one is encouraged to verbalise one's thoughts in speech or silence, whereas meditation requires a stillness of the mind to enable one to attain a deeper level of consciousness and go within oneself.

While meditation is practised in Western countries, its origin, like other esoteric matters discussed, comes from Eastern traditions. This is worthy of mention because the established Church has embraced meditation while displaying reluctance to accept other beliefs and practices from the same area.

Relative success in meditation is not easy to accomplish as it requires much concentration to prevent one's thoughts from wandering at a time when relaxation of mind is sought. A graduate from a school of meditation in the East has given testimony to the fact that a few moments of undivided attention in the process after a lengthy training period is to be congratulated. So, welcome news for all who try hard.

Anyone wanting to become involved in meditation in a serious way would be best to locate a bona fide group to join. This advice is not only applicable to meditation but to all other practices mentioned in this book, whose intention is to inform and not be a manual of self instruction. Personal tutorage from qualified and experienced practitioners is regarded as being of utmost importance. This can take place on an individual basis or in groups.

A period of meditation is sometimes included in programmes of wider variety in spiritual and metaphysical teaching establishments. These are sometimes based on what has been said above or are of a guided nature where the leader will take one on a mental journey of discovery. As has already been said, the practice of meditation will also be found in some churches and, possibly, other places of a religious order.

There is a form of Christian meditation in which a mantra of a couple of words in Aramaic is continually pronounced, these loosely interpreted as 'Come Lord'. This may be an effective method for many, as it will tend to exclude other thoughts from the mind with constant repetition of the chosen words. A quiet and silent mind may suit others, allowing unwanted and extraneous thoughts to depart and permitting stillness of the mind as much as is possible, with opportunity for any thoughts which do enter to be of a spiritual nature.

A suggestion which may be found useful in helping to still the mind and aid concentration when attempting to enter into prayer of meditation might be that of at first trying to focus the mind on one's gentle breathing and so reduce the thoughts of worldly matters other than any which may be germane.

Just relax, avoid heavy breathing, and breathe quietly and gently at all times.

Relaxation is almost a therapy in itself and often precedes the commencement of teaching activities where a 'letting go' of tensions developed is important to the process concerned. This can be accomplished on one's own by quietly and slowly relaxing the self by working progressively from the tips of the toes and up through the body to the crown of the head, drawing in Light if you wish as you go. Before starting, if you are new to this procedure, check with the advice in Grounding and Protection, chapter 26.

Visualisation is a term that one may come across in the areas of relaxation and meditation. As the word suggests it is the practice of following events in your mind's eye when all else is still, or picturing a symbol on which to concentrate steadily during meditation.

Thought forms: a discussion on Prayer and Meditation may not at first seem to be the most appropriate chapter in which to introduce this topic but having offered a reminder earlier about the need for positive thinking at all times it is as well to include it here as anywhere else, whether or not one prays, meditates or whatever one does.

It is reckoned that while thought forms originate from the same source, they manifest themselves in different ways. There is the form where the vibrations of an individual's thoughts are able to influence the thoughts of others unknowingly, or otherwise, purely by mental projection. Remember? 'Energy Follows Thought', meaning mental, spiritual and psychic energy, not just the kind it takes to swing a 14lb hammer (6.4kg).

The other concern is where some of the less attractive thoughts of the many may find their way into the Astral at its lower level and float around like flotsam and jetsam ready to engage with the minds of living souls whose guards are very well down. These examples may not be of everyday concern for all but are worthy of mention.

Where meditation and relaxation are concerned one may occasionally come across the subject of brainwave functioning. Here we are back to a dominant pillar of all life –vibrational frequency. There are a number of modes in which the brain may be found to be operating, depending on its state of activity at the time, these ranging from a frequency around 0.5Hz or less, to 40Hz or more (hertz or cycles per second, as explained earlier).

These modes of function have names which follow the frequency range in descending order:

- 'Beta' – around 12Hz to 40Hz: representing normal daytime consciousness.

- 'Alpha' – around 7.5Hz to 12Hz: deep relaxation or light meditation mode.

- 'Theta' – around 4Hz to 7.5Hz: subconscious level for deeper meditation and light sleeping.

- 'Delta' – around 0.5Hz to 4.0Hz: slowest frequency, deep sleep, unconscious mind.

- 'Gamma' – over 40Hz: more recently considered frequency suggesting a possible high functioning state of mind.

It will be seen that, apart from the Gamma frequency, the others, following through from Beta to Theta, indicate a deepening of the consciousness alongside a slowing of the mind, a process assisting relaxation and meditation as well as helping to relieve stress. 'Letting Go!' being the course of action to take. Arriving at the Delta level, one is more likely to be asleep.

20

WHERE'S GOD?

W hy are there so many wars, and why do atrocities take place? people ask.

Sad and serious being the consequence of situations which elicit such questions, heard often enough, an in-depth look into the matter from a spiritual point of view is clearly warranted.

Humankind dwells on a planet which is said to be the 'Only Planet of Choice', meaning that throughout the length and breadth of the cosmos we are the only ones with 'freewill' – maybe as an experiment. A statement of this kind obviously raises a further question: 'Why us?' To which the answer is, of course, 'Why not us?'

Then, who tells us that this is so? It is information coming to us from other worlds which are seemingly in advance of us but have less or no freedom of personal responsibility.

Planet Earth was designed as a sphere of beauty to be populated and enjoyed by all in the image of God; until things began to slide, when developing humankind, having been uniquely granted freewill, began to use that freedom in ways detrimental to their well-being.

Physical development and exploration in all possible ways led to competitiveness which, in time, led to the desire for power over fellow beings, which led in turn to greed and corruption. These negative values would obviously soon destabilise normal and secure living, leading inevitably to crime, inhuman acts and war. Do we recognise anything familiar here in the present time of living?

As already explained, God has granted every soul with every accompanying spirit the opportunity once created to keep moving forward, to evolve over any amount of time to reach perfection and return to source as part of the hierarchy. Humankind on its journey with unique freewill, acting individually or collectively, has to experience and learn for itself what is simply called right and wrong.

Despite the terrible events which do occur in the physical world it is for mankind only to sort matters out for themselves, otherwise the plan of God to allow every soul to evolve fully in its own time would not work.

God never placed a gun in anyone's hands and does not condone unspeakable acts in warfare, of terrorism and crime. God does not disadvantage the poor and lowly for the benefit of the rich and powerful; it is humankind itself which is responsible, no matter how otherwise one may feel.

Having regard to what has been declared here, each one of us is blessed by God by having our own personal spirit guides and guardian angels to watch over us all the time, offering a safeguard as much as is possible within our individual life plan. One is encouraged at all times to listen within to their own quiet inner voice, and this may well be influenced with good advice by those watching over us, but take care to ensure that the thoughts come from a positive direction and not the other way.

There is an anecdote which has been around for a while based on an idea for which we obviously cannot claim originality, except for the considerable amount of 'spin' put on our version of the story of a kind we have used for many a year. In another form entirely a very brief version has been known to have been included in a church sermon.

There was a man living on the south coast of England close by the sea. Never having thought much about the spiritual life he suddenly became aware of God in his life whom, he was told, would save him. Filled with the joyous news he went hurrying down to the end of the pier one morning to drink in the wondrous dawning of the day.

In his exuberance he unfortunately forgot to stop at the end of the pier and fell straight into the sea. Being early in the day there was nobody around when it happened, but then mysteriously a man appeared from nowhere and threw him a lifebelt attached to a length of rope. "Thank you," called out the man in the water, "but there's no need to bother; God is going to save me," and allowed the lifebelt to drift away.

A while passed and up close came a small inshore boat. "Ahoy," came a voice from the boat, "you'll be all right now."

"Have no worry," said our man in the sea, "God will save me," so after getting nowhere the boat moved off.

Now, neither the man who threw the lifebelt nor the one in the boat had been idle as a result of the victim's intransigence; both had independently alerted the Air Sea Rescue squad which despatched a helicopter that arrived later on the scene. Down on the rope descended the man from the air. "Hang on to me tight when I get near," he called out.

"No need," said our friend in the water who was now beginning to tire. "God is going to save me." After much remonstrating the airman went back up to the helicopter, knowing there was nothing more that could be done.

Inevitably the life of the dear man in the water expired and he duly arrived at the gates of Heaven as angry as anyone could be. Welcomed by the man at the gate, in spirit, our man said, "I've no time for small talk, I want to see God."

"I'm afraid that's not possible," came the reply.

"I want to have a word with God," was the demand, again. "Where's God? I'm told God is there for everyone; why can't he see me?"

"I don't know," said the attendant, "I'm only looking after the gate, but I've been given strict orders that nobody can have an audience with God until further notice."

"Then why is that?" enquired the new arrival.

"Well," said the old hand, "I can only tell you what I've heard on the grapevine. I can't vouch for it but I'll share it with you. It goes like this: God is way behind with His work and schedule of appointments; He spent half the morning trying to save some poor wretch from the sea who, it is said, stubbornly refused to be rescued. It appears that the victim was offered a lifebelt, a boat and a helicopter; what more could the fellow have expected?"

The object of this tale being: 'Recognise the Signs'.

21

THE HOLY BIBLE

The Bible is a book of words held sacred. It is also a book of history, a book of law and a book of the customs of its time, ranging over a period of anything between around 2,000 and 7,000 years ago.

The production and very existence of the Bible, which was to become available for all to read, is a matter of history in itself containing as it does texts handed down from pre-Christian times, the 'Old Testament', and then books written much later, in or about 100 years from the time of Jesus, the 'New Testament' or 'Covenant.'

Jesus the Christ died upon the cross as absolution for the sins of humankind and for teaching how one should live the good life. How much of that story in its detail, along with all the recorded happenings in the entirety of the Good Book, might not have been handed down to humankind but for the vision and courage of those men who like Jesus stood out from the crowd to be vilified sometimes for their efforts.

In those early days, reading and writing were vested in the hands of the clerics, the scribes, which was just what the establishment of that age wanted and for more than a millennium afterwards, until along came great men to change the situation forever and put the Bible in the hands of the ordinary people – the lay public.

It was Martin Luther (1483-1546), well known for nailing his edict to the church door at Wittenberg, leading eventually to the German Reformation in 1530, who translated the original Bible text into German rather than using the Vulgate Latin version. Other European editions followed.

There had been early attempts in England to translate parts of the Bible into English, among these being that of John Wycliffe (c 1329-84) who translated from the Greek. For his various works he was condemned as a heretic in 1415, after his death.

William Tyndale (c 1494) was responsible for translating the New Testament into English from the Greek with the support, it is said, of Luther and Erasmus. For his activities, ostensibly developed from his sympathy with the 'New Learning', he was persecuted and put to death in 1536. His full English Bible was produced in 1537.

Miles Coverdale (1488-1568), who it is reckoned knew Tyndale in Hamburg in 1529, published the first full Bible in English in the year 1535.

The work of each of the above named, as well as

contributions from others, finally went into the production of the King James Bible in 1611. This traditional version is used for verses quoted within this book and is still used by many today, except where the New International Version (NIV) and New Standard Revised Version (NSRV), as well as others, have taken over.

A previous chapter was given over to an understanding of how we might be able to gain a perspective of our place in the grand order of things by focussing on the brief amount of known or recorded history of the world when set alongside the age of our planet. It would not be unreasonable to suggest that the Bible encompasses the earliest part of that history, occupying a period of 4,000 to 5,000 years before, and shortly after, the time of Jesus.

In the 16th century, James Usher, a distinguished man of scholarship and an Archbishop, gave us the 'long accepted chronology of Scripture, the Creation (of the world) being fixed at 4004 BC'. This date, accompanied by an alternative figure of 5411 BC by Hales, appeared in editions of the authorised Bible for centuries to follow (see later).

In whatever way those dates may fit in to modern understanding, they begin to offer a clue to the thinking of man not so very long before our time. As appears on the diagram when we place them alongside other events, known or assumed within that epoch, there may have been little around to contradict their beliefs. (See chapter 5).

We have re-introduced the historical consideration at this juncture because, again, it illustrates how young the present civilisation appears to be when consideration is given to the fact that there is little or no known information of our society to be found beyond the earliest dates on the diagram. There are ancient fossil findings, artefacts and cave art but some of these could readily have come from the times of any other number of civilisations which once inhabited the Earth.

What the Bible has to say for some speaks for itself and may require little or no explanation; others opt to engage in a form of Bible study, maybe within a group or following other disciplines. Then there are those of the opinion that it is coded with important messages of an occult nature requiring interpretation, and this has resulted in publications specialising in such information likely to be found within the Bible. The choice of the word 'occult' here may cause a degree or two of uneasiness, not because the word or its true meaning should be a problem but because of the improper connotation placed upon it. This matter is mentioned again in chapter 26, 'Grounding and Protection'.

The word occult, like the word esoteric, simply means hidden. In fact a dictionary definition includes words like mystical and esoteric, together with explanations like 'involving the supernatural' and 'beyond the range of ordinary knowledge'. This information is offered to allay concerns when approaching the wider spiritual life so that one can be relaxed and comfortable in the presence of the ancient mysteries.

In the chapter on Religious Considerations, attention was drawn to the miracles and acts of healing performed by Jesus. Also mentioned in the chapter on Birth, Death and Passing Over was the loosening of the silver cord when departing this life. These being just a very few examples of the extraordinary amount of knowledge available to us in the Bible if we are prepared to assimilate it as an aid to everyday understanding and living.

There are straightforward examples of psychic activity appearing in both the Old and New Testaments as can be understood in the present age.

In 1 Samuel 28, the witch of En-dor is asked by Saul, who appeared in disguise to raise Samuel from the dead in order that they might speak, even though Saul had previously forbidden such things. In today's parlance this might well be referred to as necromancy, a practice not to be encouraged. Occasionally an enquirer might ask a medium if they talk to the dead, to which the answer by a genuine sensitive should be along the lines that they communicate only with Spirits from the Light who come to help humankind with its spiritual well-being, spiritual philosophy and matters spiritual in general. Divination of a fortune-telling kind is outside the scope of this work, although sought by many.

It is important to stress here that communication with the afterlife depends very much on attitude and what one is seeking. A negative approach can well produce a negative result, whereas a healthy and positive attitude can elicit a healthy and positive response from helpers in Spirit. What needs to be remembered here is that 'Energy Follows Thought'. Where self-worth is concerned we are likely to be what we think we are; also, we are capable of drawing to ourselves those things upon which our thoughts dwell. The answer to this is, therefore, to engage in positive thinking at all times. This will be discussed again later.

An event of exceptionally great importance is reported in Acts 2 of the New Testament when at the time of

Pentecost the apostles were filled with the Holy Ghost and spoke in tongues (other languages). Others, mocking, suggested they were full of new wine but Peter told them they were not drunken as it was only the third hour of the day, and reminded them of the words spoken by the prophet Joel in Acts 2:17:

'And it shall come to pass in the last days, saith God, I will pour out of my Spirit upon all flesh: and your sons and your daughters shall prophesy, and your young men shall see visions, and your old men shall dream dreams.'

The last days may be considered to be with us now, not necessarily in a cataclysmic sense but in an irreversible change of direction for the world. The old way has gone never to return, just as happened over 2,000 years ago when the Church was formed as a result of the Pentecostal event. As from 2012/2013 we are now in the new Aquarian age of 2,000 years or more duration, with all the promise and possibilities that lie ahead. There is turmoil, but after the ravages and fire comes cleansing.

Those involved in today's spiritual and psychic world have witnessed phenomena of the kind described above from Acts 2, that of speaking in other tongues, known as 'glossolalia'. We report, for example, a demonstration held for our benefit by a lady from the public, not otherwise involved in activities of the kind, who on going into an altered state of mind spoke volubly in a language completely foreign to her. There was little doubt among those listening that there was fluency in the words used and in no way were they contrived for the occasion, even though it was not possible for the language to be identified.

There are other mentions of tongues in the Bible, and, of course, the ability of mediums to receive and deliver communication from the realm of Light, whether in normal or altered tongues, needs to be regarded now as part of their everyday activity.

In fact there are first-hand reports of the singing in tongues in unison taking place in some churches, each person singing according to the nature of the tongue (language) gifted to them at the time, all tongues coming direct from God.

We soon come to Self-empowerment: opportunity to set oneself free from restriction.

James Usher, who lived between 1581 and 1656, and John Hales (1584-1656) were by the reckoning of today's understanding more than 4.5 billion years out in their estimations, but for their time the answer was anybody's guess when it is realised that eminent scientists as recently as the end of the 19th century were fixing the planet's age anywhere between just 20 million and 100 million years old. See next page.

It was due to the introduction of radiometric dating in the 20th century that the present level of knowledge has become available.

See also chapter 5, 'Historical, Evolutionary & Spiritual Perspectives'.

CHRONOLOGICAL SUMMARY OF BIBLE HISTORY FROM THE CREATION OF THE WORLD TO THE DESTRUCTION OF JERUSALEM

THE PRINCIPAL EPOCHS IN THE BOOK OF GENESIS ACCORDING TO THE DATES GIVEN BY USHER AND BY HALES.

USHER. Before Christ.	Year of the World.	EVENTS.	HALES. Before Christ.	Year of the World.	USHER. Before Christ.	Year of the World.	EVENTS.	HALES. Before Christ.	Year of the World.
4004		The Creation	5411		2233	1771	Dispersion of the descendants of Noah (Usher)		
3874	130	Birth of Seth	5181	230					
3769	235	Birth of Enos	4976	435					
3679	325	Birth of Cainan	4786	625	2247	1787	Dispersion of the descendants of Noah (Hales)	2924	2787
3609	395	Birth of Mahaleel	4616	795					
		Death of Adam (Hales)	4481	930			Birth of Serug	2354	2857
3544	460	Birth of Jared	4451	960	2185	1819	Birth of Nahor	2492	2919
3382	622	Birth of Enoch	4250	1122	2155	1849	Birth of Terah	2283	3128
3317	687	Birth of Methuselah	4194	1287	2156	1878	Death of Noah (Usher)		
3130	874	Birth of Lamech	3937	1474	1998	1996	Birth of Abram	2153	3258
3074	930	Death of Adam (Usher)			1996	2008			
3017	987	Translation of Enoch	3914	1487	1921	2083	Abram arrives in Canaan	2078	3333
2948	1056	Birth of Noah	3785	1656	1896	2108	Birth of Isaac	2053	3358
2348-9	1656	The deluge	3155	2256	1836	2168	Birth of Jacob and Esau	1986	3418
2346	1658	Birth of Arphaxad	3153	2258				1885	3526
2311	1693	Birth of Salah	3018	2393	1775	2276	Joseph goes to Egypt		
2281	1723	Birth of Heber	2888	2523	1706	2298	Jacob and all his family go to Egypt	1863	3548
		Death of Noah (Hales)	2805	2606	1689	2315	Death of Jacob	1816	3265
2247	1757	Birth of Peleg	2754	2657	1635	2369	Death of Joseph	1702	3619

YEARS B.C.	EVENTS IN THE HISTORY OF THE ISRAELITES.		CONTEMPORANEOUS PERSONS AND EVENTS IN HEATHEN COUNTRIES.
1699	Birth of Moses.		
1619	Departure of the Israelites out of Egypt.		
1579	Moses dies. JOSHUA.		CHUSAN, king of Mesopotamia; EGLON, king of Moab; JABIN, king of Canaan; &c.
1557	Joshua dies. From that time till 1150, OTHNIEL, EHUD, DEBORAH and BARAK, GIDEON, ABIMELECH, TOLA, JAIR, JEPHTHAH, IBZAN, ELON, ABDON, SAMSON.		
1153	ELI.		NAHASH, king of Ammon.
1119	SAMUEL.		
1090	SAUL.		
1057	DAVID reigns at Hebron; and ISH-BOSHETH at Mahanaim.		HIRAM I. (Abibalus), king of Tyre; HADADEZER of Aramzobah; TOI of Hamath; HANUN of Ammon.
1050	David reigns at Jerusalem over all Israel. Prophets Nathan and Gad. David brings up the ark, and places it in Zion; extends his kingdom from Egypt to the Euphrates.		PSINACHES in Egypt: HADAD and GENUBATH in Edom (?); REZON in Damascus.
1017	SOLOMON succeeds. Prophet Nathan.		HIRAM of Tyre; PSUSENNES II. in Egypt.
1014	Commencement of the building of the temple.		
1007	Completion of the temple; and beginning of the palace-building. Prophet Ahijah.		
977	Solomon dies. Division of the kingdom.		SESOSTCHIS (Shishak), in Egypt.
	Kingdom of Judah.	Kingdom of Israel.	
977	REHOBOAM (reigns 17 years). Prophet Shemaiah.	JEROBOAM (reigns 22 years). Prophet Ahijah.	
973	Jerusalem plundered by		Shishak.

219

＊H＊

A page from an authorised version of the Bible circulating in 1894 quoting dates of the creation of the world according to Usher as being 4004 BC, and Hales as 5411 BC.

22

SELF-EMPOWERMENT

Having reached this stage in our disclosure of the reasons for why we are all on Earth, we have to accept that there are some, and probably many, who would unhesitatingly declare that they do not believe a word of what has been said. Yes, we meet them only too often, but before we give the impression that we might be downhearted the boot, as we say, is on the other foot.

Alas, if we should be heard to be sighing it is not for us but for those who throw away their golden chance when the opportunity is placed before them. Not that our business is in that of conversion; it is to inform, as pointed out much earlier. The information available is that of a highly specialised nature, one might say of a privileged level, and it is not thrust upon anyone. It is available purely for those who are receptive to the ideas and knowledge.

Experience shows that those for whom our words will resonate tend to come forward with agreeable anticipation in order to know more. There are others who, without prior discussion on hearing of this work, unhesitatingly lose no time in loudly articulating their disbelief of the whole process as though they are programmed for whatever reason to object. This is something to which workers in the field are quite accustomed and reminds one of sound advice coming from Spirit: 'never push against a closed door'.

There are so many souls now in incarnation who want to know more that time cannot be utilised on those who are not yet ready; their time of flowering may be many incarnations to come, but that time will come for them.

'The harvest truly is great, but the labourers are few: pray ye therefore the Lord of the harvest, that he would send forth labourers into his harvest.'
Luke 10:2 (Matthew 9:37-38)

For those going forward many doors will begin to open. To begin with there is the 'moment of awareness' to be reached. Some may be on their way to it, others might have reached it – 'the expansion of the consciousness' – when one's views of so much hitherto held and taken for granted can be turned upside down and assume different complexions.

Self-empowerment can now come forward if it has not been dominant of late. In the envisioned attic of your house – your mind – a trunk is stored which needs to be unlocked. A key is needed; YOU are the key! Your application, dedication and flowering enables you to access the trunk in which is stored layers of knowledge and wisdom – the Ancient Wisdom – built up from any number of former incarnations and journeys to the Light. That information will not necessarily be readable at the moment of unlocking, but as its meaning becomes apparent you can become empowered to proceed with absolute confidence in and with the knowledge that you are a child of God, an emissary of the Light, who is able to carry that Light with them, remembering always that it is an awesome responsibility to carry the Light.

What you need to know at this stage of your spiritual journey is already with you and will come to the front of your mind as you move forward. If you are truly ready you will become as absorbent as a sponge in respect of what you hear, read and notice in the way of spiritual realisation, spiritual unfoldment and spiritual philosophy. Your life is capable of being changed forever at this juncture, but take care: while there may be a thirst for knowledge to accompany your new way of life, there are no shortcuts. Progress can be accelerated and you may want to get on with it quickly but there is usually an adequate amount of time ahead.

As you open up you may begin to see and perceive things differently from some of your friends and neighbours, but as long as your intentions are pure and honest then hold on to your new-found truths and beliefs. Be prepared to stand up and be counted because there are a great number of doubters, disbelievers, ignorant and frightened people out there who will argue and do their best to dissuade you from your true course. The would-be detractors can easily and unwittingly serve the negative aspects of life eternal so be positive on all occasions, as has been previously advised.

Don't try to change the thinking of the obstinate and those who want to take you on in an argument. You are aware of your truth while they, yet, have to find theirs. On the other hand be ready to help those who come forward with a genuine desire to learn. One soon learns to identify the different types of enquirers.

Hang on in there and the rewards will be yours. It is said that the angels weep for those who turn back from their pathway; Live in the 'Light' and Live in the 'Now'. Remember yesterday but don't hanker after it. Have vision for the future but don't live for tomorrow. If one clicks one's fingers, that moment has come and gone. Has it really been lived in? Will it ever come again?

With self-empowerment comes energy to do the job in hand. Coming up soon to our chapter on Spiritual Healing we are now in as good a place as any to touch on the need to hold on to the energy level and watch our health, for which unseen micro bacterial assailants and others are eagerly awaiting an opportunity to slip in and devastate – as soon as the guard is dropped – when the immunity system is reduced or depleted.

This can happen, of course, whether or not one is working on their spiritual quest, but having prepared and worked on one's development for a worthy purpose one does not want the result to be undermined without having made a worthwhile effort to resist.

Into a category of things to be kept under review will

obviously be over-indulgence in all things, among which will be hardy annals like smoking, excess drinking and drugs. Stress from over-activity whether in work or play is better avoided; failure to look after the self properly and insufficient rest and similar features which might inhibit the body to safeguard itself are obviously to be avoided.

The next step is to discuss Mediumship.

23

MEDIUMSHIP

Let us first give thought to the fact that mediumship in the present age is so different from any impression of what it was like in the first half of the 20th century and earlier – the days of darkened rooms, round tables, white sheets, planchettes, trumpets and all the other apparatus associated with the practice; a setting of a kind one might see in a film of the period.

Mediumship in the form of spiritualism took shape in the mid-19th century in the USA before arriving in the UK, although it might be assumed there was always an element of the practice somewhere around. It was the age of silent rooms, rapping on tables, lights moving about, hoarse voices and ectoplasm, and claims from sceptics of fraudulent behaviour. Perhaps there was some skulduggery here and there but current practitioners have a lot for which to thank the grand old pioneers because of the foundations they laid for later development. Anyway, those days are gone, except perhaps for the unwise and the dabblers who enter the water beyond their depth, which we stress is not to be recommended. It is always better for novices to enter the water when the lifeguards are on duty – just to be sure.

Transition into a fast-moving pace of life in a rapidly changing world over the last half century or more in most areas of human activity, and now the digital age, means the old ways have given way to a polished spiritual and psychic profession realisable on both sides of the great divide.

Mediumship now covers quite a range of activities which could be supposed by the unknowing to be supernatural and beyond worldly understanding. The situation could not be more different. As we have attempted to explain, the totality of the life eternal is around us all the time; all levels of life in Spirit interpenetrate our space and beyond at their particular level of vibrational frequency. The higher the level the more is known, the more is seen, and we on Earth are at the lowest functioning level, so here is where mediumship comes into its own, by offering the process of communication with higher levels in the Light – 'the other side'.

If we substitute communication for mediumship, for the moment, we can then deduce that communication itself will take many forms and these will be explained. First, however, it will be useful to run through some fundamental considerations.

The word 'medium' means just the same in spiritual and psychic terms as it does when used in any other capacity, simply – intermediary – 'in between' – 'in the middle'. So, in our case, the medium is interposed between those on Earth and the active communicators in the Light who work with the medium to bring forth knowledge of all kinds that would otherwise be denied us, including that of the ancient mysteries.

It is necessary now to distinguish as best as possible between spiritual and psychic activities. Our explanation for this is that a person can be very spiritual without being the least bit psychic and can be psychic without being very spiritual. Both often go together, each being a gift that can come naturally or be developed to an extent, but always, we stress, it is the spirituality of the person which is the main factor in their personal development and evolution of their soul. Certain mediumship work is more likely to be considered spiritual, while other may be taken to be especially psychic.

A list of psychic practices and spiritual therapies carried out by mediums of one speciality or another can be quite exhaustive. It is our intention, therefore, to restrict the discussion to what we consider to be the main areas of interest.

Just as in most professions the nature of the medium's speciality can be dictated by the demands of the clientele. A principal example of this is where those normally in communication with Spirit, at a level from where spiritual truths and philosophy are kindly provided for the benefit of humankind, will probably be less liable to be found working in a situation where the regular demand is for evidence of survival. An example of this is where a bereaved person seeks news of a loved one passed over.

Mediums may also be described as 'sensitives' or 'instruments'; the client is sometimes described as the 'sitter'. A session with a medium may be called a 'sitting', occasionally a 'reading'. The following explains the main forms of mediumship, and spiritual and psychic gifts.

Clairvoyance: The faculty of a medium to see things beyond normal perception. Derived from the terms, *clair*, meaning clear, and *voyeur*, meaning sight – to see. The medium is able to view emanations appearing around the sitter such as from their aura or from visitors in Spirit form (apparitions). Discernment is with second sight, not one's normal sight.

Clairaudience: Where the sensitive receives aural communication in his inner senses from those in the world beyond, which may be for his personal information or for that of the client. Derived, again, from their meaning *clear* and *audient*: to listen – to hear.

Clairsentience: Following on from what is explained above, this means the medium may become aware of the presence of unseen visitors and thereby receive an indication of what troubles the client. Derived from *sentient* – to perceive and to feel.

Precognition: This is inserted here as it has been known to be mistaken for clairvoyance with, perhaps, other of the above abilities. It is where the person who may or may not be a practising medium can see or has knowledge of events yet to take place – a form of seer.

Psychometry: As with the immediate above, this is placed here because of its similarity to clairsentience. It is the ability to obtain a sense of connection with a person by feeling and handling possessions belonging to that person in their absence.

Trance: A condition where the medium allows his own spirit to move aside and permit his body be occupied by a working partner from the Spirit world. In this capacity, information of a spiritual/psychic nature can be given direct to the client.

Channelling: A satisfactory form of mediumship for the age. It has been likened to a lighter side of trance, except that the instrument (medium) is not taken over. A companion in Spirit closes in upon the medium and communicates information direct to the higher self of the medium by the action of thought, which is then conveyed instantly to the sitter (client), or whoever, in the normal language of the medium.

Tongues: These have been discussed in the chapter on The Bible where in The Acts of the Apostles 2, the apostles are filled with the Holy Ghost and speak in their own language instead of the local vernacular; this is not unknown in our time.

Guided Writing: Many great books have been published for our benefit as a result of this gift where the writer receives a continuous flow of information from their communicator in Spirit through one of the methods described.

Automatic Writing: Similar to above except the medium's arm, hand and, thus, pen is under the control of the spirit guide producing valuable information. Needless to say, all these processes are entered into with the full and willing compliance of the instruments concerned. Some processes will also be seen as variants of the main forms of mediumship.

Scrying: A form of divination well known but the reason is not always understood. It is where the medium concentrates their gaze on a crystal ball or other object in order to aid their concentration while seeking information.

Psychic Portraits: The medium having artistic ability is guided by Spirit in a process which quickly produces a picture of the attendant spirit for the benefit of the client who is sitting before them. This is sometimes accompanied by the receipt of messages from the spirit self. There are good psychic portrait artists around but it is our wish to draw attention to the work of the late Coral Polge. Psychic portraits produced for the author in the mid-1990s by Coral appear in this book.

Dowsing: Surprisingly, perhaps, water divining and other forms of divination with material instruments come into this category, especially the use of the pendulum, which is well liked by many. A pendulum comprising a crystal on a small chain resembling a piece of jewellery can be quite popular, but any reasonable small artefact on a piece of string might do just as well, as the ability to obtain answers lies very much in the user.

The list of lesser known and more specialised spiritual and psychic activities, together with associated therapies and ancillary matters, continues on but we will mention just a few more of particular interest, not to forget Palmistry, Divination Cards – the Tarot, and others.

Materialisation: Often regarded in the past as the work of stage magicians, objects and even people have, nevertheless, been known to have left one place and materialise in another by paranormal means under the direction of a mystic. The process of movement in these circumstances is known as teleportation and the objects are referred to as apports. In this category of activity there is also the ability to receive ash, known as vibuti, from out of thin air into the palm of the mystic's hand. In a similar way, oil can appear into the hands of a medium.

Transfiguration: The ability of the medium to introduce the features of Spirit, an attendant, possibly on to their own face or that of another. An advanced process needing much energy it can usually be brought about by intense concentration by the medium on the other person.

Before concluding this chapter we feel it worthwhile to add a few further words on the subject of the early years of psychic activity compared with the more current spiritual approach, as pointed out in the opening paragraphs of this chapter.

Meetings held for those interested in the psychic phenomena, roughly during the period of mid-19th to mid-20th centuries, would be held during a séance, which meant that a circle of people including a medium or two would sit in a darkened room, with the object of connecting with the near departed, more likely to be at some level in the Astral.

An instrument of particular use during these meetings might be that of the planchette, which was invented at the beginning of the period by a French citizen, M. Planchette. This would consist of a piece of boarding with castors for mobility and a pen attached so that held lightly by the medium and under the motivation of spirit presence the board could move about and produce messages by guided writing.

It has been claimed that this might be an instrument of very ancient origin and can in some ways be likened to the Ouija board, which has not received mention here so far as it is not an instrument we would recommend to be in the hands of unskilled and inexperienced operators.

A particular aim of a circle when sitting was to cause a manifestation to appear, this being brought about by a substance called ectoplasm, to emanate and give recognisable form to the visiting spirit. Ectoplasm is a cloudy Etheric-like matter, which is reckoned to exude from the operating medium, sometimes from the mouth as well as other parts. An earlier medium of celebrity standing divulged to a fellow worker of high regard how her solar plexus area was heavily bruised from working in this field of activity. A therapist/spiritual worker engaged in massaging a client was left with a large handful of this substance in her hand!

This information is to aid in the wider understanding of the immensely wide coverage of the subject matter as a whole and is not an endorsement for anyone to attempt to follow these – by and large – superseded practices, although they may well continue in places.

Modern spiritual practices work at a much higher and greater level, as will be understood from the contents of this book, bringing much needed teachings for the benefit of humankind.

There is a major spiritual practice we have left to the end so that it can go forward into its own chapter, this being Spiritual Healing, which is also a form of mediumship, as will be explained.

It needs to be qualified that all who employ their gifts and engage in these activities do so by the grace of God, the Father, Son and Holy Spirit, and all who come in His name. See 1 Corinthians 12:1 and 4-10 in the following chapter on Spiritual Healing.

PSYCHIC PORTRAITS

The portrait above and those on the pages which follow are selected from the work of the late Coral Polge, gifted psychic artist, all sketched under spirit guidance for the author personally during separate sittings at the then headquarters of the Spiritualist Association Great Britain (SAGB), Belgrave Square, London, over the years 1992-94.

One would be invited to sit comfortably alongside Coral Polge, with her sketchpad, crayons and other essentials close by, and then off she would go sketching briskly, accompanied by a running commentary of whatever communication might be coming in along with the guidance of her hands, all from unseen help in the world beyond.

Three quite separate and individual portraits intended solely for the sitter were produced in one hour, that is twenty minutes for each sketch with whatever detailed work was required.

The portraits are intended to bear the likenesses of family members, friends, colleagues, teachers, mentors and all with whom the sitter might have had personal connections in this and previous lives.

24

SPIRITUAL HEALING

S piritual healing is a highly regarded form of service and mediumship. Healers are mediums because they, too, are interposed between spirit activity in the Light and humankind they serve on the ground. Many healers also share in some of the spiritual and mediumistic gifts already described.

> Now concerning spiritual gifts, brethren, I would not have you ignorant…
> Now there are diversities of gifts, but the same Spirit.
> And there are differences of administrations, but the same Lord.
> And there are diversities of operations, but it is the same God which worketh all in all.

> But the manifestation of the Spirit is given to every man to profit withal.
>
> For to one is given by the Spirit the word of wisdom; to another the word of knowledge by the same Spirit;
>
> To another faith by the same Spirit; to another the gifts of healing by the same Spirit;
>
> To another the working of miracles; to another prophesy; to another discerning of spirits; to another divers kinds of tongues; to another the interpretation of tongues…
>
> 1 Corinthians 12:1 and 4-10

It is a privilege to perform as a healer as, indeed, it is to operate with all gifts granted by God. And that statement spells out an important message, which is that all who wish to serve and do God's good work should do so with humility, respect and responsibility.

A question sometimes asked is: 'How does healing work?' The answer to that can be very simple on the one hand but quite complex on the other, so we'll offer a straightforward example, on the basis that accomplished healers have usually developed their own style of working through belief and experience.

The healer who is endowed with God's gift operates as a channel between healing companions in the Realm of Light – Heaven – and the one who seeks healing – the client. The healer of experience asks God and those who come in His name from the Light if he or she (the healer) may offer themselves as a channel for the divine rays of healing light from the Godhead to come through them for the benefit of the client. The healer also asks the higher self of the client if it wishes to accept the healing and on receiving positive responses all round unites with the collaborating team in Spirit.

Depending how the individual healer works he, or she, may place their hands a little way over the client's head and feel the energy coming through to the client, possibly around the area of the pineal gland. The healing energy, the healing light, will go to the areas of the client requiring attention, the client usually feeling the process working within and around them. Alternatively, the healer might place their hands near to each of the client's seven energy centres on the body (Chakras – see diagram) as well as to any area where a specific problem is realised or reported.

The whole process may last from about five to fifteen minutes. On completion, the healer should give thanks to God and all who came in His name, and possibly to the higher self of the client. The client should then be closed down: that is to prevent the energy centres remaining open after the process is finished – protection.

Absent Healing: Spiritual healing is also offered in the absence of the patient who may be in a location far removed from the healer. Employing this technique has even allowed the healing effect to be experienced at a distance halfway around the world from where the healer was positioned. Customarily, those for whom the healing is intended are usually nearer to hand. An 'Absent Healing List' of those seeking help is maintained by some healing organisations allowing individual or collective treatment.

It is emphasised that these explanations are for interested enquirers who ask how the healing works. They are not intended to be a self-help set of instructions. As will be realised there is a great deal of learning coupled with experience before a trainee, probationer, can become a fully fledged healer – usually around two years.

It needs to be explained, as well, that not all healers by any means operate in Anglican church locations where there, or anywhere else, one pays homage to God as the Supreme Being. As mentioned much earlier, some healers and others working in spiritual service within the community tend to acknowledge the healing energy as being Natural Healing coming from the Universal Consciousness, or similar.

The Healing Fellowship at St Mary-le-Bow was originally founded as an autonomous group in January 1995 under the then rector, the Rev'd Victor Stock, later the Very Rev'd Victor Stock, who when leaving for higher office in 2002 was succeeded by the current rector, the Rev'd George R Bush, who by warm agreement enabled the healing meetings to continue.

Pure spiritual healing as has been practised and taught at the church for 20 years is suitable for physical, spiritual and emotional conditions. A particular interest has been that of offering healing to the soul from where so many problems originate. Applied at this level the healing energy is also able to reach other locations it may want to treat.

A form of healing worthy of mention here is that of Reiki healing from an Eastern tradition which became popular here from around the end of the 20th century. Those who follow the practice speak well of it.

Crystal healing is a well-established practice, sometimes accompanying spiritual healing. The energy from gemstones is used to effect the healing of a patient (chapter 7).

Self healing and animal healing are also carried out. There are other types of healing practices, too, but our concern is with the major forms of Spiritual Healing, in which, ethically, a healer must not offer, promise or guarantee to heal or cure any specific conditions or adversities affecting a client (patient). Both healer and client are in the hands of the Lord and His will provides that which is necessary for the situation.

Spirit Release: A procedure allied to Spiritual Healing except that the object is to free the patient from a spirit that has become attached to them while at the same time guiding the released spirit to the Light. There is also Spirit Rescue where unattached discarnate entities can be helped to the Light. These are both highly specialised operations and quoted here for information purposes only. They are mentioned again in the following chapter on Grounding and Protection.

As a supplement to this chapter on Spiritual Healing the following examples extracted from earlier in-house publications are offered to provide an indication of what can be achieved. The words used are predominantly those of the contributors and no personal claim is made for the results shown, most of which may be described as fairly typical of what should be expected in a responsible, bona fide, healing and teaching practice.

"Geoff Thomas, our healer... offered me healing today. In silence and without touching me, a weight was lifted and I felt clearer, lighter and happier as the day went on. It was strange and inexplicable, but welcome." (VS)

"…I nodded and the next 10-15 minutes of healing certainly changed my life… I felt incredibly calm; the turmoil and heavy lead weight within my chest seemed to 'melt' away. The emotional lump in my throat was a lot better… I thought about my experience and was deeply moved by it… I have to say that looking back it has changed me and changed my life." (HS)

"I saw the surgeon yesterday for my post-operative appointment and I haven't got ***** or anything life threatening… you were so supportive and I really appreciate that… the surgeon said they were baffled, because with their findings I should have been doubled up with pain, but I haven't had any pain, and I am sure this is all due to your healing." (DC)

"Geoff guided me through a spirit release that was beautiful, gentle and very moving… It goes without saying that one has to have complete faith in the spirit release therapist, and for me it was a very powerful, emotional and freeing experience and I am so glad and grateful that Geoff was able to help us both." (D)

"Since that day (of healing) I have not experienced any migraines, which I have been suffering from for 15 years… the wonderful feeling of peace I experienced that day… thank you for this wonderful gift. It has changed the quality of my life." (SV)

"Coming from a strict Catholic background, much of what Geoff had to say often went against all that I had been taught, yet none of it was unacceptable to me. I recognised that I was becoming more and more open to 'ideas', for want of a better word, that I had previously shunned or chosen to ignore… it is not my intention to be pompous, but I do feel enlightened." (PB – Spiritual healing and development course.)

"May I thank you for all you have done at the Healing Group. You have helped more people than you may have realised." (JW)

"My gratitude for the spiritual healing given to me… by the wonderful people at St Mary-le-Bow… All of the healers should be proud of the difference they have made to those of us who come for healing. Your sacrifice of time and patience is much appreciated. I will always remember the Crypt and the warmth of the special people there." (JS)

As indicated earlier, ethically, no promise or guarantee of a remedy or cure for any condition or affliction can be given or expected. We are in the hands of the Lord.

The following longer edited transcripts are offered to convey the help and support derived from spiritual healing by two visitors to the healing sessions.

"I don't know whether this letter will reach you, but D and I wanted to thank you very much for ministering to us and giving us the benefit of your healing powers. D's chest is still doing remarkably well, despite the damage caused by 30 years of chain-smoking (which she gave up five years ago, fortunately).

D and I took several pictures of St Mary-le-Bow, and the spiritual energy of the place was apparent even to strangers like us who are not very well versed in spiritual matters.

Thank you very much for all you did for D and me. Best wishes from both of us."

The original of this letter was sent from a lady in Germany to the main office at the church, who handed it on to the healing group. Visitors from abroad quite often attended the meetings, as did those of other faiths, or without faith.

This is the second letter. It is a longer letter, substantially edited because of the symptoms and personal information involved, but the content shown will give an indication of the help received by the sender.

"It is now about five months since I came to see you at St Mary-le-Bow for help regarding tiresome… disorders that, despite extensive medical care, had been plaguing me for a long time. During this period spiritual healing has touched my life in a real and substantial, albeit unexpected, way…

"When, at the end of last year, I started working in the City, I noticed with some surprise that spiritual healing sessions were being held once a week in the basement of the church. I had heard a lot about that kind of practice, and had seen demonstrations on one or two occasions. Since I regarded it as something bigger than me, and beyond the grasp of my logical mind, I decided to give it a try; it couldn't possibly do me any harm and would only take ten minutes once a week. I was convinced that, although it may not make me feel better instantly, sooner or later it would take at least some of my symptoms away.

For quite some time (something like six to eight weeks) hardly anything seemed to happen, except for the fact that I always felt very peaceful after a session. Then one evening something took place while I was having coffee with some friends in a little Italian restaurant… I had the impression that, out of the blue, a light had been switched on in a very dark room and suddenly I could see everything very clearly. The most remarkable thing about that particular episode was my determination 'to live' and to move forward.

In the course of the following weeks (I was still having healing on a regular basis) that special feeling persisted and actually became more intense… Even more remarkable… was an absolutely priceless sense of inner peace and calm. It didn't occur to me at the time to connect this state of things with spiritual healing… But when I couldn't come to see you for almost two months… It was only then I connected my new-found well-being to spiritual healing, and was then left in awe of that Intelligence that had touched me where I most needed it...

...I try not to take any of this for granted; my feeling is that I received a beautiful gift... I also view spiritual healing not like a course of medication to take at prescribed times, but rather like some wise source of help... I want to thank you all for all you've done to get me this far."

This abridged letter was received from a most intelligent lady of overseas nationality living in the UK.

It needs to be said that these and the other testimonials are received on behalf of all in the healing practice at St Mary-le-Bow and represent similar expressions of appreciation likely to be offered to all engaged throughout the bona fide healing movement.

There is a particular aspect of spiritual healing which, though included here, might well have appeared in the later chapter 29, 'Future Considerations'.

We refer here to Psychic Surgery, currently known or believed to be performed by a very limited number of exceptionally gifted healers. This is a practice in which the healer can carry out procedures on a non-invasive basis that would otherwise require the use of surgical instruments. It is not possible to comment on the efficacy of this practice, although satisfactory reports do circulate.

Many of us have reason to be thankful for the skill of the surgeon operating upon the body physical on an invasive basis with customary instruments, and we will continue to be grateful for a while to come, but one cannot rule out developments in medical science proceeding at such a pace that advanced forms of surgery may eventually seem to be not so entirely different from those of the Psychic Surgeon.

An objective of this book has been to demonstrate how young our present society is when put into context against the history of our planet. Orthodox medical practice, as we know it, developed from the time of the Barber Surgeons in the Middle Ages, can be considered as being remarkably young, evolving all the time.

Spiritual healers are privileged to work with sacred rays emanating from the cosmos through the intermediary of spiritual guidance. Can we not visualise the surgeon and medical practitioner of the future operating with such rays or similar, whether of natural origin or induced by electrical means? The use of X-rays has been with us for some time now and laser beams are increasingly used for medical purposes. There must surely be an age to come when the surgeon's knife, along with the daily dose of medication, will be committed to history.

Sci-fi? We think not!

It is well realised that medical science, like other branches of science, is developing at a prodigious rate; being capable, no doubt, of keeping pace with the rapid growth in global population.

THE CHAKRAS

Energy Centres

The name of each centre is followed by a few brief words about its better known characteristics and connections

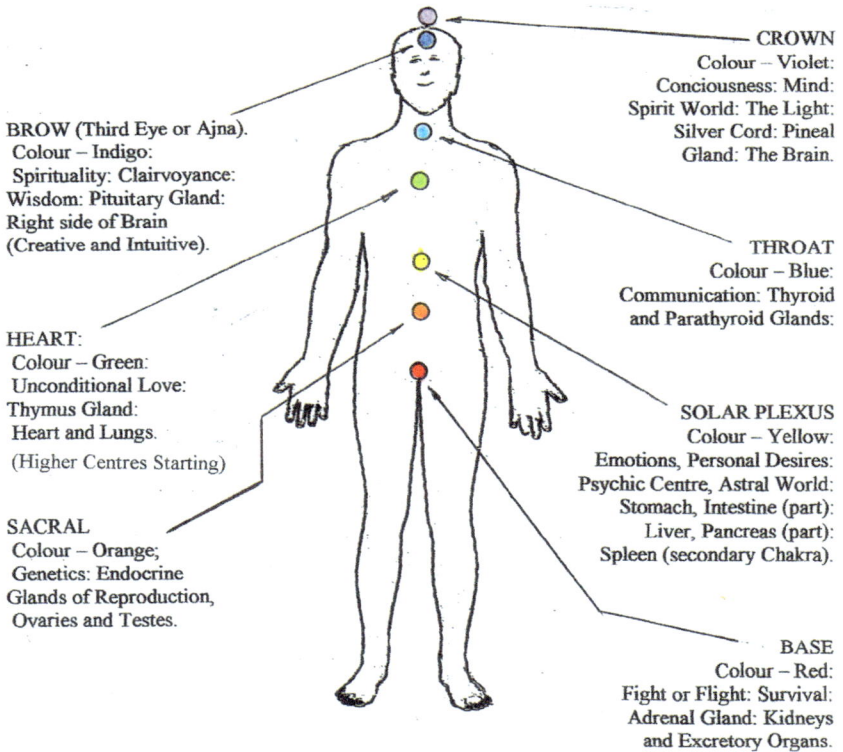

CROWN
Colour – Violet:
Conciousness: Mind:
Spirit World: The Light:
Silver Cord: Pineal
Gland: The Brain.

BROW (Third Eye or Ajna).
Colour – Indigo:
Spirituality: Clairvoyance:
Wisdom: Pituitary Gland:
Right side of Brain
(Creative and Intuitive).

THROAT
Colour – Blue:
Communication: Thyroid
and Parathyroid Glands:

HEART:
Colour – Green:
Unconditional Love:
Thymus Gland:
Heart and Lungs.
(Higher Centres Starting)

SOLAR PLEXUS
Colour – Yellow:
Emotions, Personal Desires:
Psychic Centre, Astral World:
Stomach, Intestine (part):
Liver, Pancreas (part):
Spleen (secondary Chakra).

SACRAL
Colour – Orange;
Genetics: Endocrine
Glands of Reproduction,
Ovaries and Testes.

BASE
Colour – Red:
Fight or Flight: Survival:
Adrenal Gland: Kidneys
and Excretory Organs.

155

Chakra is a Sanskrit word for wheel; in this case a spinning wheel acting as a vortex aligned over each portal – energy centre – enabling healing energy to enter the holistic body. It may be noted that the colours associated with each centre follow in the same order as those of the spectrum of light (see chapter 15) where they progress from red at the base centre of lower vibrations up to violet with the higher energy and, hence, greater frequency of vibrations at the crown centre.

The generally understood locations of the Chakras shown here may be regarded as ones of a primary nature as others, like the spleen, are termed by some as secondary. A similar notation might also be applied to Energy Centres not so closely allied with the physical body, such as those of a higher level function, not usually shown, above the crown.

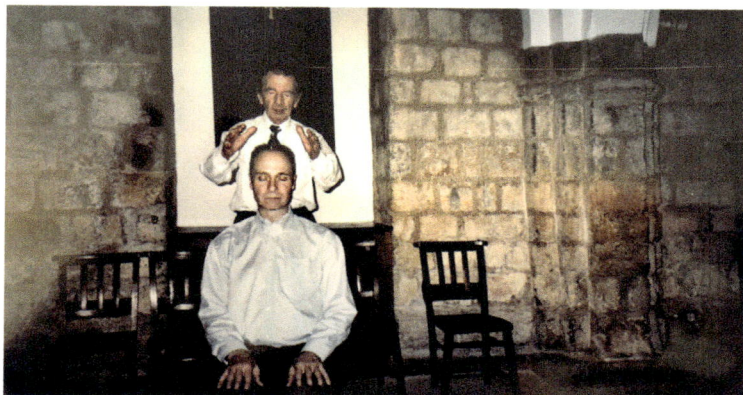

SPIRITUAL HEALING

A demonstration of Spiritual Healing performed in the Crypt Chapel of The Holy Spirit at St Mary-le-Bow Church in the City of London. The picture shows the author, Geoff Thomas, inviting the healing power of the Holy Spirit upon fellow healer, Mark Lewis.

By kind permission of the rector, churchwardens and PCC, the Healing Fellowship at St Mary-le-Bow held regular public meetings at the church from January 1995 until September 2015, when there was a moratorium to allow building operations to proceed within the premises. Teaching programmes in Spiritual Healing, as well as to facilitate Spiritual Development (Realisation and Understanding), also took place during this 20-year period.

After more than 20 years continuous and uninterrupted healing and teaching meetings at the church, the Healing Fellowship has now wound down its activities, thus permitting the retirement of its leadership to become engaged in other directions.

25

NOTHING NEW
UNDER THE SUN

Staying with the practice of spiritual healing, what needs to be told at this juncture is not only a remarkable account of a form of healing carried out many years ago but also the gateway it provided toward the preparation and publishing of this book. (This follows from chapter 2, 'The Call'.)

The dramatic expansion of complementary and alternative therapies during recent decades might well invite us to enquire: "But what happened before then?" As far as healing is concerned we know that Jesus was, and is, the greatest of all healers, and we are aware that forms of healing will have been practised since time immemorial.

But what of a seemingly quieter period nearer to the

present; in the first half of the 20th century, for example, when the current general awareness and practice of healing was much less known and the great pioneer Harry Edwards had not yet published his original *Guide to Spiritual Healing*, to be followed by his definitive version some 20 years later: *A Guide to the Understanding and Practice of Spiritual Healing*.

Around the turn of this century a letter from our good friends, the late Tony and Anne Alexander, was received, together with a copy of a Sunday newspaper, *The People* published way back in 1935. It was sent to acquaint us with an article at the top of the front page of that newspaper which reported on the amazing healing work of Mrs Amber Sparkes, an aunt of Tony's.

Relaying this event to members of our healing and spiritual group I went on to explain the close connection between that newspaper's most respected columnist of the time, Hannen Swaffer, and Maurice Barbanell, the highly regarded medium for the communications from spirit guide Silver Birch whose messages and teachings of wisdom and spiritual understanding have been of immense inspiration to so many.

Hannen Swaffer, a former doyen journalist of Fleet Street and one-time editor of *The People* – Sunday newspaper – conducted a spiritual and psychic home circle which included a previous young sceptic, Maurice Barbanell, who experienced a complete psychic transformation before going on to become a most renowned medium during a lifetime of spiritual service, including the founding of *The Psychic News*.

In a later chapter mention is made of the frequency of

communicators from the spirit world choosing to appear as being of Native American origin. The possibility here being, among others, that the communicator might well prefer to choose this form close to our own time and understanding, whereas forms from other lifetimes might just as easily have been selected.

As mentioned above – and told in chapter 2, 'The Call', – the intervention of a message from Maurice Barbanell in spirit has been instrumental in the writing of this book.

Returning to Aunt Amber, Mrs Amber Sparkes, what follows is a complete transcript of the news item about her and her work, together with a part copy of the front page of the revelant newspaper, *The People* dated Sunday 30th June 1935.

WOMAN WHO HAS X-RAY EYES

SHE CAN SEE THROUGH THE BODY HER AMAZING POWER TO HEAL EXCLUSIVE TO "THE PEOPLE"

Woman with the X-ray eyes. That is the only way to describe Mrs Amber Sparkes. Her eyes possess the extraordinary faculty of being able to see through flesh and bone, so that the secrets of the human body are exposed to her gaze.

A Bournemouth osteopath, Mrs Sparkes employs this unique gift to aid her in her work. A patient goes to her surgery to consult her. After listening to an account of the complaint, she will gaze searchingly at the patient. "There is a small bone displaced at the base of the neck," she will say. "From what you tell me it is probable that this is due to the fall you had as a child. Bend over and I will put it right for you." With a few deft touches of her hands, the trouble of years is put right in as many minutes. How she came to take up healing is a romance in itself. Herself a sufferer from rheumatoid arthritis for many years, she was cured in an unusual manner.

Doctor after doctor had treated her in vain. At last, a friend persuaded her to see an osteopath. So effective did the latter prove that this woman, withina few weeks, was able to walk about again.

Strange Romance of Healing

So impressed was Mrs Sparkes with this treatment that she determined herself to take up this work of healing, to which she had had a leaning ever since a child. Now her fame is world-wide. So great is the demand for her services that she is only able to attend to a selected list of patients.

They come to her from all parts of the world, from Australia, South Africa, the United States, Kenya, China, Japan, India and even the South Sea Islands.

Recently she saw a gypsy woman in the garden of her villa. She went out and told her to go away, as there were already plenty of flowers. "But," this woman protested, "I didn't come to sell you flowers. It is my face."

Mrs Sparkes looked. The gypsy woman was suffering from extreme neuritis. "But what made you come to me?" she demanded. The woman looked at her. "I don't know," she answered, "except something kept saying to me: Go to that house. You will be cured."

She begged Mrs Sparkes to put her hands on the affected part of her face. The latter did. A few days later the gypsy came back again, full of gratitude, to say that the neuritis had been completely cured.

Courtesy of Trinity Mirror Publishing Limited

Gift Discovered by Accident

It was by accident that Mrs Sparkes discovered the unusual property that she possessed in her eyes. She was massaging a patient when, suddenly, to her surprise, she found herself able to see right through her body. It was not the bones and muscles so much as the all-important nerve centres that were exposed to her view. She is unable to explain this queer gift.

It is not her physical healing

that she regards as of primary importance, but the cures she has effected with mentally deranged patients.

A perfectly healthy young woman suffered from an hallucination. Every morning when she woke up at seven o'clock she went mad for a few minutes. Her madness took the form of being afraid of being left alone, and insisting that the room must be crowded with people.

One morning Mrs Sparkes went to her house just before seven. The woman appeared to be perfectly normal. Then, suddenly, at the usual hour a look of complete madness came over her face.

As she looked the healer seemed to see behind the woman the scene of some Eastern land. There had just been a great earthquake. Later, when the patient had become normal again, Mrs Sparkes told her of the vision that she had had.

"It's all right," she assured her. "You were in great peril at that particular moment, but the danger can never overtake you now. You must put it from your mind."

The woman did. Today she is completely cured.

Whilst it might be argued that there is more often than not an element of psychism working alongside the spiritual, as in the remarkable process demonstrated above, what is to follow is a fascinating example of how the two processes came to be operating jointly but severally during a healing procedure.

A normal and regular spiritual healing session being

conducted at St Mary-le-Bow was found to give audience to a long departed soul who engaged the attention of a lady receiving the healing treatment. What follows is the report provided by the lady, generally as written.

"On Monday 31st March I visited St Mary-le-Bow Church in Cheapside London. I met with Geoff, with whom I had some healing.

The healing took place in the crypt of the church. During the healing I saw a lady called Marion. She was well dressed, in a dark green dress with a large square neck. She wore a gold coloured metal chain with a cross that hung to the right.

Marion was a very young, slim lady with bright red curly hair. She was standing behind me praying towards the altar. The image of the crypt cross was also different to that of how I viewed it on my last visit. During my visit the chairs were laid in a circle but in Marion's time there would have been pews. There were candles/torches on each pillar; the area although dark was well lit.

I followed Marion up some wooden stairs (through an entrance which no longer exists) into her own private dwelling. It was possible to enter the house without having to go outside; Marion was walking through the building. She led me to some stairs, which I was too scared to follow her up. She repeated her name to me twice, as though to almost comfort me, but I still refused to follow.

After the healing I spoke with Geoff and asked him if he was aware of Marion and her house. The house no longer exists and is now an office block.

Concerned with what I had seen, I searched for Marion and I came across some information.

1434: Marion was the widow of Thomas Malton Esq, who resided in a house bounded to the east by Hosier Lane. 1464: She married John Rotham, alias Rodom. 1465: John leaves Marion an interest in his will to continue to reside at the house until she dies.

I also researched the fashion of this era to confirm I had the right Marion.

My personal interpretation of this is that Marion will always continue to reside in her house and to serve the church."

AUTHOR'S NOTES:

A brief check on the research carried out by this enterprising lady tends to suggest a degree of reliability with regard to the people involved and the description of the area around the church in the middle 15th century; this being 200 years and more before the Great Fire of London (1666) which devastated the City of London as it then was. Further investigation shows that Hosier Lane was on the east side of St Mary-le-Bow Church, with Goose Lane on the west side, before the fire took its toll on the church, then to be rebuilt by Sir Christopher Wren. This is able to explain why Marion could possibly walk direct from the crypt into her home; the crypt, incidentally, being the only part of the church to survive the fire.

There is still a Hosier Lane in the City, this being in the Smithfield area and not to be confused, quite obviously, with that from the 15th century of the same name.

This account takes us back to our concern over the comment made by the presenter in the scientific radio programme mentioned in chapter 1, the Introduction, when using a ghost passing through a solid wall as a metaphor added, "If you believe that sort of thing!"

The story rightly supports the title of this chapter, 'Nothing New Under The Sun'. It goes back over 500 years and is by no means an isolated case within the church or anywhere else.

The crypt of St Mary-le-Bow is of most historic importance, being of Norman origin – after Roman London – and has survived the Great Fire as well as World War II, when most else was lost. It has been an immense privilege to be able to conduct regular weekly spiritual healing meetings in the crypt chapel over a period of 20 years, during which teaching courses in healing and spiritual development were also included for a good part of the time.

Visitors attending the meetings would often speak of the energy, peace and quiet to be found there; it is a special place and acknowledgement is made to the many who made their way to the meetings and to the healers there to greet them.

Thanks are due to the clergy and churchwardens, Parochial Church Council, church staff and others for enabling the Healing Fellowship (the Healing Group) to carry out its work so efficaciously during the period concerned, January 1995 to December 2014.

26

GROUNDING & PROTECTION

W hy do we need protection if the spiritual life is so good for you? Good question! Well, you could liken it to raising your umbrella when it's raining to avoid getting wet. It could also be suggested that going to your gym for a healthy workout is most beneficial for you but if you're crossing a main road on the way and forget the rules of the road, looking neither right nor left before stepping out, then there's a good chance you'll finish up in hospital. A bit of a grim picture but you get the idea.

Having respect for the things that can trip you up, and then taking appropriate care in advance, is paramount in most, if not all, avenues of life these days, and it's just the same with spiritual and psychic activities. But, as we have stressed several times, our words are to inform, not teach. Personal tuition, individual and group, in the practices mentioned in this book, is available throughout the land.

Operating in the Light, maintaining good positive energies and paying attention to your protection should present little problem, but just as on this side of life there are some doubtful characters, much is the same on the other side. As told through an advanced medium many years ago, "If someone is pushy on this side, they will be likewise on reaching the other side." Meaning, don't expect that they might change and become saints overnight.

This statement offers a useful timely reminder that not all souls who have gone over are comfortably settled in the Light, for the reasons given earlier, and while not being of malevolent disposition can be a nuisance for the unwary. The practices of Spirit Release and Spirit Rescue mentioned in a previous chapter provide examples of discarnate entities in need of help, as well as the affected human beings.

One is familiar, no doubt, with stories of greater concern, which are surely just as likely to manifest themselves among members of the general public as with anyone else. The situation here is not being helped by the plethora of so-called supernatural and horror films, loved by the TV and film industries and those who watch them, which draw negatively to themselves and to the places from where they are viewing.

There are one or two suggestions that can be offered, however, that may make things a shade more comfortable for all on the rocky road of life.

We have talked a fair amount about the Light, that is the Celestial Light which exists in abundance but is normally unseen in this life. That Light is there for you. How? You might well ask. By visualisation is the answer. Close your eyes (not mandatory but useful) then visualise scintillating white light around you and within you. When do we need this? Perhaps when you're sitting or standing in an overcrowded train or bus with a feeling of negativity around you. Maybe when you get home from your day's activity rather jaded because, like the situation on the train, you have been absorbing negative energy – or, in fact, any other time you feel the need for spiritual cleansing.

Cleanse your aura with the Light. In your visualisation bring down the wonderful Light, run it through yourself and return it to the place from whence it came, complete with the negativity you've cleared away.

By now you might be wondering how to find the Light. And this is where we return to a point made earlier. By using the Mind. 'Energy Follows Thought'. The mind is powerful and enables you to create your own reality, not make-believe. We have said earlier that the mind is of the soul/spirit and it is the means of communication with the spirit world during the present life and in the afterlife.

If you are feeling particularly uncomfortable in a crowded or unpleasant environment, try drawing your aura closer into the physical body by thought process and by surrounding yourself with Light, because at any time the aura may be well extended and mixing with those of some murky customers. Again, this is the sort of thing that can happen to anybody, whether or not they are involved in spiritual work.

An unpleasant truth but hopefully not surprising to many is that one's vulnerability to unpleasant psychic interference increases with excessive alcohol and drug intake, and over abundance of mortal pleasures. This is not a morality warning – that is not our business – it's because waiting in the Lower Astral on the other side are some beings who have departed this life with a craving for such indulgences. They are just waiting to pounce when the opportunity presents itself. A similar situation can occur when former members of the low life on earth will be ready to jump in where elements of criminality are involved. In both examples they are finding a home for their passions.

We stress here that this concern is only with the absolute excess of behaviour in these activities and there is little doubt that those who engage in a normal way of life with ample social enjoyment will be unaffected by the situation.

It is also necessary to stress that concern about discarnate entities (free-floating spirits in limbo) and spirit attachment with possible help from Spirit Rescue and Release specialists is not to be confused with the state of Spirit Possession, a matter requiring particular specialist help when met. Needless to say, this should be avoided at all costs, hence the advice given.

Remember, the higher the development of one's spiritual energy – frequency of vibration – the less likely one is to be affected by lower and sometimes negative energies.

Grounding is simply a matter of keeping one's feet on the ground, which should not be a problem after our much earlier words on the effect of gravity. But this is different, as we have since discussed a good deal about the spiritual life where Mother Earth, supreme as she is, is the first step – the first level – in our eternal journey. So at any time when relaxing with a view to prayer, meditation, or starting any spiritual exercise, cleansing with the Light or feeling vulnerable in any way, just sit and feel your feet well placed on the ground with legs uncrossed.

The term 'ground' means any floor surface on which one is standing, even if it's many storeys up in a high-rise building; we're back to thought process so if needs be you can be in bed. Visualise roots going down, down and down from the soles of the feet until you see them rooted in the earth below. You are now grounded, earthed, or anchored if you prefer a nautical approach – it's all a matter of using the mind. When ready, bring the mind back from the exercise, draw yourself together, have a few deep breaths then continue with whatever task you'd set yourself, or just remain relaxed.

In the matter of safeguarding oneself, which is the thrust of this chapter, without wanting to over emphasise the need and give rise to undue concern, it is an appropriate place to bring together aspects of likely situations even if already touched upon.

The kindly ones are those dealing with the passing of loved ones, or anyone revered, where every effort needs to be made to let them go forward on their spiritual journey and not be held back by those left behind. Love transcends the frontiers between lives here and in the hereafter, just as though there were no barriers, so why deny progress of loved ones in the finer realms and maybe cause them to take up unseen residence in their former dwellings due to the strength of the pull from physical sources on Earth?

A situation of this kind can also operate in other ways. One is where those passed over do not want to leave Earth behind of their own volition for all manner of reasons, including a situation like that of the above – of not wanting separation from a loved one. Another is in less kindly circumstances such as where a lifetime or less spent on alcohol, drugs and gross earthly indulgences can instil a desire to remain behind as a discarnate entity in order to continue to enjoy the fruits of the former passions.

Mention has already been made elsewhere of souls earthbound and in limbo, and possibly unaware of their true circumstance because of former life choices such as ignorance or wilful refusal to accept a life hereafter and what that encompasses. They may hang around for a time in no-man's-land until getting their bearings or being assisted forward by helping hands on either side of the great divide. No limit in Earth time can be placed on the waiting period during which their presence may occasionally be experienced on this side of life.

Situations of an experimental or adventurous nature in matters of the occult likely to produce similar results are best avoided except under the close and supervised direction of a qualified and experienced tutor. There is reference in chapter 21 to concern over the use of the term 'occult', which for some has a sinister ring due, presumably, to a lack of understanding over its true meaning which, like the word esoteric, simply explained, means hidden knowledge.

So, there is good occult and bad occult, just like good and bad in anything, but the meaning of the word seems to have acquired a reputation for the negative rather than the positive.

The message here is that if one is confronted with the result of any of these or similar situations it is possible to seek advice from helpful organisations and individuals if the matter persists.

What follows is a diagram in concept intended to illustrate how, by raising one's vibrational frequency in terms of spiritual development, anyone can help themselves to keep clearer of the darker forces coming from the shadow side.

HOW PROTECTION CAN WORK FOR YOU

This is a model in concept only.

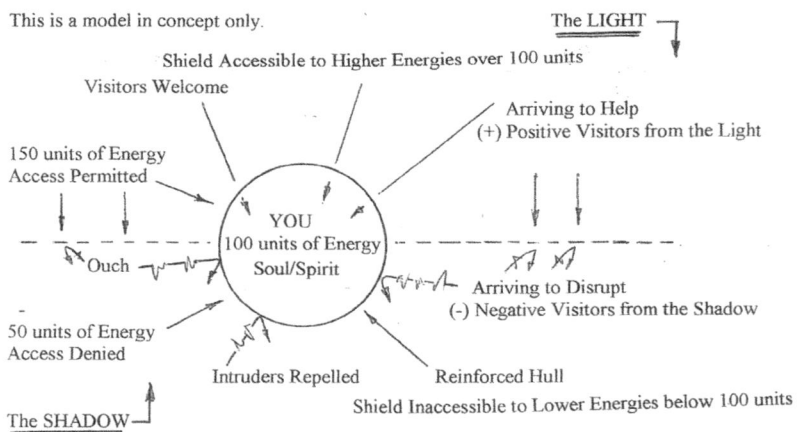

The LIGHT

Shield Accessible to Higher Energies over 100 units

Visitors Welcome

Arriving to Help
(+) Positive Visitors from the Light

150 units of Energy
Access Permitted

YOU
100 units of Energy
Soul/Spirit

Ouch

Arriving to Disrupt
(-) Negative Visitors from the Shadow

50 units of Energy
Access Denied

Intruders Repelled   Reinforced Hull

The SHADOW

Shield Inaccessible to Lower Energies below 100 units

The purpose of this diagram is to show that the higher the frequency of one's soul/spirit vibration, hence energy, the greater is the amount of protection afforded from unwanted low-level, shadow side, intruders. The possibility of such intrusion exists even if one is not involved in the spiritual life, except that in such circumstances one is likely to be quite unaware of the reasons for some of the problems which have come upon them.

So it is worthwhile pressing on with the raising of one's personal vibes by dint of homage to God, entering into prayer and meditation, studying spiritual realisation (which this book affords as a starter), thinking positively, getting involved in personal service, being a power for good and, above all, being ready to believe the unbelievable. If you are not already on the pathway, these are just a few suggestions; what is important is that you will become aware of what is needed: opportunities and priorities will speak for themselves – don't let the chances slip by.

Returning to the diagram, and as has been explained already, energy as a result of vibrational frequency can only flow from a body of a higher energy level to one of a lower level and not vice versa. That is why the beneficial visitors from the Light shown as having 150 units of energy are capable of accessing us at our lower 100 units level, while the unwelcome visitors from the Shadow at 50 units are denied entry to us.

This demonstration is purely conceptual and the energy values selected are for comparative purposes only, with no other validity here.

In certain spiritual and psychic work the sensitive (medium) will purposely engage in allowing, even encouraging, entry of lower level spirits into their own domain in the practice of spirit release and spirit rescue; helping attached spirits and discarnate entities (lost souls) to enter the Light. Needless to add, these are tasks to be undertaken only by experienced specialists.

27

UNCONDITIONAL LOVE

As the title would imply, it signifies that one seeks to ensure the well-being of another without expectation or anticipation of receiving a similar act in return – although it would be nice to have.

Not that we consider ourselves necessarily qualified to advise on such a delicate and personal subject but it remains, nevertheless, that as we draw nearer to the end of this guide on the wider implications of the spiritual life we might not be completing our task if we did not draw closer attention to the Golden Rule which is, or should be, applicable in all the major religions and avenues of belief.

From the Sermon on the Mount in the Holy Bible, Jesus said:

'Therefore all things whatsoever ye would that men should do to you, do ye even so to them: for this is the law and the prophets.'

Matthew 7:12 (Mark 6:31 is similar)

That Christian version of the Golden Rule spoken by Jesus has connections with statements in the Old Testament, and is simplified in current language to:

'Do unto others as you would have them do unto you.'

A fuller version, The Great Commandment, is based upon an account of a Pharisee lawyer tempting Jesus by asking him:

"Master, which is the great commandment in the law?"

Jesus said unto him, "Thou shalt love the Lord thy God with all thy heart, and with all thy soul, and with all thy mind.

This is the first and great commandment.

And the second is like unto it, Thou shalt love thy neighbour as thyself.

On these two commandments hang all the law and the prophets."

Matthew 22:35-40 (Mark 12:28-31 is similar)

The quality of unconditional love drawn from these exhortations may inevitably be harder to exercise on occasions than should ideally be the case.

In everyday life one can be confronted with issues of wrongdoing and this, touching upon the antonym of love, means we are in the area of hate which doubtlessly comes into the category of sin capable of taxing decent human emotions to their limits.

Sin has been very well defined as 'the absence of love'.

Those who are prepared to cause harm and distress to their fellow beings in whatever way, and seek power and possession over the interests of their companions, then that according to our book must be interpreted as sin – anything from the taking of a life to the robbing of the poor box. And the definition has to be extended to include harm against the animal kingdom and all the kingdoms of God wherein wanton cruelty exists.

Here we are reminded of the seven deadly sins: lust, gluttony, greed, sloth, wrath, envy and pride, the meanings of which need no explanation.

Now, into the theatre of love, hate and sin, comes forgiveness, balanced against the desire for revenge. There is no more telling a quotation than that attributed to Confucius, Chinese philosopher, 551-479 BC.

'Before you seek revenge remember to dig two graves.'

Francis Bacon, 1561-1626, said: 'A man that studieth revenge keeps his own wounds green.'

Our words, again, are not offered as an attempt to preach but as an understanding towards that which helps advance one's spiritual development on the inclined pathway.

Among the leading desirable components helpful

in assisting the forward movement of one's spiritual development must surely be that of one's positive attitude and consideration for all fellow travellers on the accompanying journey – to accord dignity, love and respect for all human and sentient beings with whom we share this planet, which can be quite extensive when we take into account all that comprises the Kingdoms of God as shown on the diagram of that name at the end of this chapter.

An aspect of unconditional love which should not be overlooked in the interest of all protagonists is the unwillingness, the refusal, to offer forgiveness.

How often have we heard the expressions: "I'll never forgive" or "I might forgive but I won't forget". It may seem very hard, even uncaring, to say that they who utter these remarks risk delaying their progress on the spiritual journey and possibly exacerbating emotional damage already sustained, even if the innocent victim of a dastardly crime or grieving for one who has been. Yes, it's easy to say this but it needs to realised as a distinct possibility.

Failure to let go can continue beyond the grave and become a block to the spiritual progress of victim as well as perpetrator, holding both hostage due to an inability in the one to forgive and in the other to repent for sins committed. A situation of this kind can hold fast for the equivalent of any number of lifetimes until satisfactorily resolved, but with eternity at one's disposal the problem is not as acute as it would be on Mother Earth.

As is pointed out elsewhere, the guilty in this life will need to compensate for their actions on the other side even if they are not brought to account in this life; such understanding can offer comfort to any who find it difficult to grant a natural forgiveness.

'Forbearance and forgiveness, however hard, brings spiritual strength and growth.'

'To err is human, to forgive, divine.' Alexander Pope (1688-1744)

'Humility may be introduced here, remembering that it is the meek who shall inherit the earth.'

This chapter has been very much about attitudes and emotions; welcome and desirable traits when of positive orientation but negative when about to expose human frailties.

An emotion which might be said to cover both aspects is that of anger, which is known to divide opinion between those who would claim that some anger can be fully justified as opposed to the alternative view that all anger is unhealthy.

We might turn to the Good Book again for a lead on this point. There is a good deal of anger in the Old Testament, much coming from no less than God himself; and in the New Testament, given over to a forthcoming era of peace and unconditional love heralded in by Jesus, we are exposed to the wrath of our saviour when he overturns the moneylenders' tables in the temple.

There are many instances in the early books of the Bible where passages refer to the anger of the Lord being kindled, an example being:

'And the Lord's anger was kindled against Israel, and he made them wander in the wilderness forty years, until all the generation, that had done evil in the sight of the Lord, was consumed...' Numbers 32:13

In the New Covenant there is:

'And Jesus went into the temple of God, and cast out all them that sold and bought in the temple, and overthrew the tables of the moneychangers, and the seats of them that sold doves...' Matthew 21:12, also Mark 11:15

No pussyfooting around in either of these instances. So, what are they telling us? Being aware of their sources, are we not looking at forms of 'tough love'? When a job of what one deems to be of a corrective nature needs to be done it has to be done, however one may feel about the consequence. And if the anger has been honest and just, then one should not be left with a feeling of guilt, a negative emotion more likely to result from unjustified and unhealthy anger risking impairment of the self-worth.

It is at this juncture we can take the opportunity to take stock of the fact that, according to deep space communications we, alone, have a choice in our decision-making. Inhabitants of our planet, alone, have the benefit of freewill because, surprising as it may seem, ours is the only 'Planet of Choice'. That is:

'While other planets do have choice, the consciousness is collective. Only on Earth can a being experience individual choice.'

Why do we want to waste such a precious gift as this, and any others granted by God?

Visualise if you will the president of the board sitting at the head of the boardroom table. On one side is Mr Light with his team alongside, on the other side Mr Shadow with his team. The president says, "Right, gentlemen, off you go and do your best."

You see, we have a choice. Why not take it? There may never be a better opportunity.

KINGDOMS OF GOD

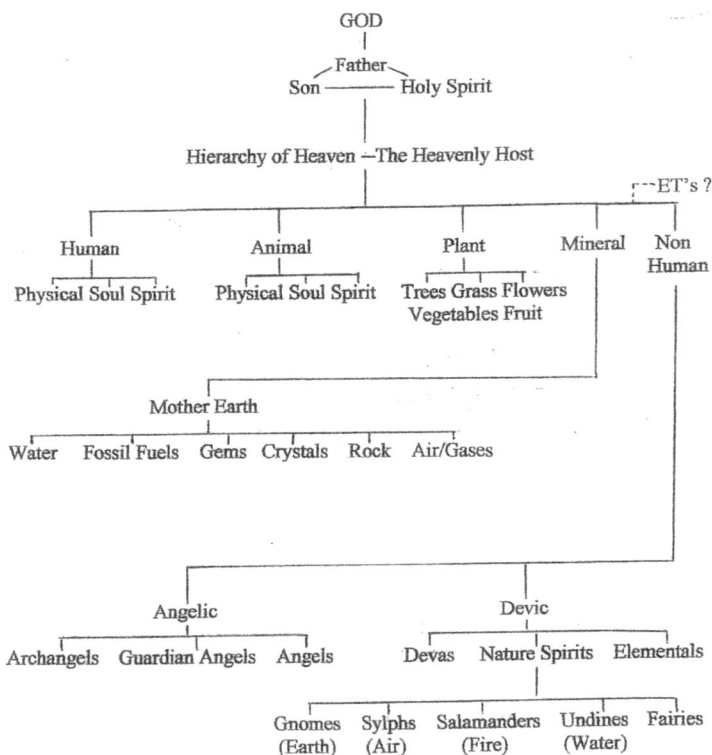

GOD
|
Father
Son ——— Holy Spirit
|
Hierarchy of Heaven —The Heavenly Host

ET's ?

Human · Animal · Plant · Mineral · Non Human

Physical Soul Spirit · Physical Soul Spirit · Trees Grass Flowers Vegetables Fruit

Mother Earth

Water · Fossil Fuels · Gems · Crystals · Rock · Air/Gases

Angelic · Devic

Archangels · Guardian Angels · Angels · Devas · Nature Spirits · Elementals

Gnomes (Earth) · Sylphs (Air) · Salamanders (Fire) · Undines (Water) · Fairies

A suggested arrangement of constituent members of the Kingdom of God of which other and many alternatives might be offered. The object here is to show the many aspects of His Kingdom and how they can be said to relate on a spiritual level.

All in the Kingdom of God have a soul. All are 'ensouled'.

28

BALANCE

'Let me be weighed in an even balance, that God may know mine integrity.' Job 31:6

This is a topic which might well not have got its own clear space within this book and could easily have received a mention tucked into one of the many other chapters.

But the need to obtain balance in all areas of life is of such great importance – and never more so than when discussing religion, spirituality, faith and belief – that in our opinion a separate section is warranted to highlight the significance of any concern.

It would be only too easy for a person with a deeply committed faith of whatever persuasion to hold a view that no other pathway of understanding can share in the divine ordinance of God. There are many avenues along which one can travel, all leading to the same destination at the end of the day.

It is many a millennium since the scriptures in the Old and New Testaments were written – not very long in the annals of time but a lengthy period on a generational basis.

While the words of Jesus and the Apostles were intended as a set of rules, or guide, on how one should live in any age, they were, nevertheless, directed at the people – especially the transgressors – of that particular time. Is it not possible that the tenets delivered then might have since been changed, updated, to reflect the advanced level of civilisation and development now current in areas of education, culture, arts and sciences, interplanetary exploration and so forth? Like other considerations within this book it may be worthy of a thought!

The exercising of one's judgement in orderly decision-making is one thing to consider but the act of being hasty, judgemental and intolerant in the conduct of fellow beings is another. The reason for another person's beliefs, attitude and behaviour, which may not accord with our own or the norm as we perceive it, may be known only to God: Father, Son and Holy Spirit, and the Hierarchy of Heaven.

Balance in all of one's deliberations is paramount for Christians and all faiths, and for those professing to have no faith at all.

An area sometimes dubious in this quality is that of the media, by reason of the service it is expected to provide. Headline – grabbing news one day might cause the public to adopt a jaundiced opinion of a person, only to find later that the news – previously speculative – has now been turned around to provide that person with a clean sheet– the problem then being that a little mud might have stuck.

'Moderation in all things' is an oft-quoted sentiment in everyday life which we recognise quite simply as a way to encourage the need for 'balance'. We enter this world to gain experience in the physical life, to be of service to all human and sentient life, and to make spiritual progress with such joy and happiness as may be granted for the occasion. To pursue a pathway of largely or solely personal indulgence and gratification is more than likely to be a missed opportunity. There is a choice.

Never to be overlooked is the importance of balance in the human behaviour originating in the mind, as mentioned in the chapter on 'Subtle Bodies', where through the action of the right side of the brain we exercise the intuitive, creative and feminine aspects of ourselves. On the left side, however, it is a matter of the rational, materialistic and masculine.

Expressed in this manner an answer can be offered to a question not infrequently asked: "Why do Native Americans (previously known as Red Indians) feature so often in spiritual and psychic work?"

The Native Americans who passed on in recent centuries, like Aboriginals from other parts of the world, were generally intuitive, spiritual, lived very close to nature and, it might be said, had their ears close to the ground. Western society, on the other hand, meaning those in developed nations, were on the whole engaged in materialistic and financial affairs, with little time for spiritual considerations – as is largely the case today with the rise of the (so-called) secular society.

Consider, for example, that as a result of the Industrial Revolution, from which the more advanced societies at the time gained materialistically, the workers producing the wealth laboured from dawn to dusk in grim and tiring conditions with little or no opportunity to experience a natural life, unlike those living the great outdoor life in the lesser developed or undeveloped parts of the world – however primitive that life might have been.

Those coming forward from the past are not by any means confined to a limited background, as the psychic portraits mentioned in the chapter on Mediumship show, and it is from their ranks that the spiritual teachers come to be with us. It is useful as well to realise that those coming forward, whether from Native America or from any other source, are likely to present themselves in a form with which we can identify because, having served lives on Earth previous to the one depicted (reincarnation), they could just as easily appear as members of earlier or other cultures.

If asked for a recommendation on how to achieve harmony in the human mind we could only suggest operating more on either the creative or rational side of the brain, the right or the left, the feminine or the masculine, depending where the deficiency lies, if any. By that we mean perhaps spending a little more time on creative and artistic pursuits and so forth if it were felt such needs were warranted, or vice versa if the other way around; in either case making suitable adjustments to the way of life.

Referring to the working of the brain through the mind, it may help to remember that all, that is man and woman, are fundamentally composed of male and female essences and it is advantageous to the well-being of the individual to try and maintain these in whatever satisfactory balance is comfortable for them.

To conclude this discussion on Balance it would not appear unreasonable to remind ourselves of that very important aspect of the subject already given in chapter 10: 'Karma; a state of being which is neither Bad nor Good but one of Balance; the opportunity to move through any number of lives to enhance one's spiritual evolution and move closer to the Godhead'. So, again, it seems it's up to us!

29

FUTURE CONSIDERATIONS: THE WAY AHEAD

PART 1: IMMEDIATE

The future which lies before us has several dimensions. On one level, measured in lifespans incomprehensible, it is endless; that is until the sun in its declining years will expand to a size which will engulf Planet Earth and all that lies before it. By that time humankind in its adapted form will have emigrated to other planetary realms.

Nearer to our present time we are confronted with the major problems of the day which can be the harbingers of doom for the future. There is Global Warming and Climate Change; National Fear, Avarice and Megalomania; Nuclear

Catastrophe, War and Terrorism; Population Explosion, Famine and Emigration. It is not too difficult to realise that these factors have all the regrettable properties of an inter-relationship in strife.

What is to be done about it? It is for man alone to find the way through. That is his learning curve, to lead him and all mankind to the ultimate spiritual uplands. He has his destiny in his hands. And what if mankind doesn't succeed? Well, he must; it's his choice, but if he doesn't then this civilisation will come to an end and in due time it may start all over again. So, we have a choice, God is beneficent, patient and all forgiving but, as in so many of these kinds of issues, it's up to us.

If the understanding of reincarnation was universal there might be fewer meaningful but disingenuous homilies about making the planet a better place for the generations to follow, when realised that today's man may well be returning to a quasi desolated landscape himself in his next life.

The nearest level to the future is that of the immediate; that moment after we've snapped or clicked our fingers in the 'now', the 'present', the 'moment' which has come and gone never to return, the aggregate of which is the measure of our lifetime. They are the decisions and the actions of the present which will shape the tomorrow.

It might be just too easy to believe that a word with God through well-placed communicators in Spirit and mediums on the ground would tell us all we need to know about the future. True, there are clairvoyants and other gifted sensitives who are able to give a measure of information to the individual person, touching upon their personal situations. This should be considered as guidance and advice, however excellent, and not by any means forms of instruction to be sought and acted upon, because if given and accepted the individual would be denied the employment of their own freewill and choice: precious gifts for all humankind in their development.

There may be occasions when a message of extreme urgency will reach the mind of a person either directly or indirectly when about to enter into what may prove to be a hazardous situation but such events are of a different nature from those where reliability is regularly placed on the mystic word from others. Help with decision-making can usefully come from listening to one's own 'still inner voice' emanating from the higher self, connected since coming into this life with the world of Spirit.

The higher echelons of teachers and guides from the Light, of human and angelic origin, bring messages of peace, hope and encouragement to man on Earth by way of teaching and spiritual philosophy, imparting knowledge at a heavenly level. Such communications suggest to us how our ways of living are but mirror ideas of those in the realm above, operating here at a substantially lower level of understanding and performance. Attention is drawn to the inhumanities and injustices which exist, especially those which flourish in the wake of gross materialism. The messages offer hope for the future but, no surprise, any substantial improvement will need to wait until mankind learns to change its ways, which on present performance can be a long way ahead.

Of the major problems of concern which the world faces

at the present time, and attention needs to be drawn to, is that of population explosion. Proceeding on the basis that God will not deny a place in Heaven for all who are worthy, or another place for the miscreants, it must follow that the Lord will not deny entry into this world for all newly born souls. This means we can be fast heading towards a state of overcrowding in the more habitable parts of this planet, assuming such a condition has not already been reached; so it's up to us; there is a choice.

Humankind has freewill, and if the citizens of the world can do little or nothing to ameliorate the situation, either voluntarily or by legislation, as has been attempted, the responsibility must inevitably continue to lie with man and not with God. What follows is a graph showing the incredible rise in world population in recent times: every soul living now or projected to be here in the future, being in essential need of the basic commodities taken for granted by Western civilisation – food, clothing, fresh water, healthcare, housing, sanitation, education, employment and more.

From where are the necessary resources coming? And how many more souls might there be to swell the numbers which – it might be reasonably assumed – will continue to grow exponentially unless, or until, there is massive intervention? Famine, starvation and disease, especially in arid parts of the world, have become regrettable scenes. If this is to be accepted as a major problem of our time, as well as that of the years to come, it is for humankind to start resolving the matter now.

WORLD POPULATION GROWTH
1800 AD-2050 AD (PROJECTED)

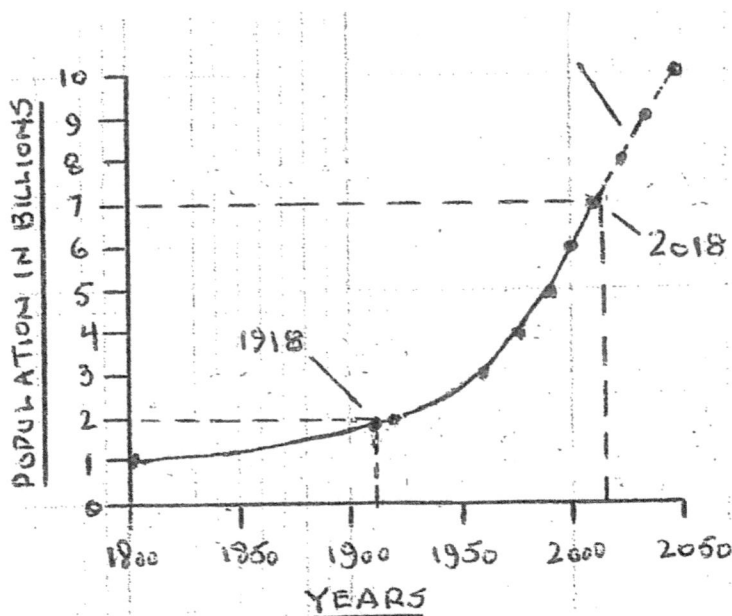

*Approximate increase between 1918 and 2018 for illustration purposes,
with rough indication of possible increase to 2050 following present rate
of expansion.*

One does not always hear of a direct connection between population growth and its deleterious effect on global warming but the following example offers a rough illustration of how global warming can be adversely affected by the continuing and rapid expansion of life upon the planet.

Examining the situation over the last 100 years which is within living memory, we find that the population around 1918 was around two billion. Compare that with the reported level of around seven billion (and maybe more) in 2018 and we can get an idea of the tremendous increase of greenhouse gases and other noxious products going into the atmosphere by reason of, at least, five billion additional human beings with their accompanying needs during this short passage of Earth time.

This unprecedented acceleration in the growth of human population is not only responsible for liberating vast quantities of additional waste heat, methane and carbon dioxide but also for an untold number of animals in support doing likewise, and then for the huge dependence on industrial processes to maintain much-needed supplies at a comparative rate.

These consist of everything from natural and processed foods to modern-day requirements – automobiles, aircraft, information technology, building construction, heating and cooling of homes, workplaces and public buildings, and so on – all contributing in turn to this vexed problem which world governments need to resolve while there is time. The internationally agreed target is a rise of 2°C; it is now at 1.2°C.

The hole in the ozone layer which can allow unacceptable

levels of ultraviolet radiation to reach us is a separate matter and largely caused by chlorofluorocarbons (CFCs) emanating from refrigerators, in service or redundant, aerosols sprays and packing materials, etc. CFCs are now banned but it may be many years before the ozone layer repairs itself, and it needs to be recognised that a substantial population increase, having had considerable possession of these consumable items, will have enhanced the situation – possibly the ultimate demise of the planet together with global warming and other hazards if mankind does not keep a firm grip on the situation.

The facts and opinions offered here are intended as a guide to the infrequently heard effects of population growth on climate change. No accuracy is claimed in the rough calculations and the results if ever truly known could well swing one way or another, but the point in principle is clearly established and it is for man to think about in the way ahead.

Analogous examples sometimes help to highlight the message. For example, if one had been running a global soup kitchen around the year 1918, so that everyone in the world at the time could have one bowl of soup each day, there would have been a need for two billion (2,000,000,000) helpings per day. Come forward 100 years to the year 2018 and the need for such a service has increased by a further five billion bowls (5,000,000,000) a day, making a grand total requirement of seven billion bowls (7,000,000,000) per day: an uplift of 250%. From where is it all coming? Surely a major problem for any restaurateur!

If Armageddon were just around the corner it would probably be less likely to be coming from such possible happenings as an impact due to an asteroid or comet, or from an earthquake, volcanic eruption, tsunami, plague, wars or nuclear disaster but from global warming which is already taking effect. Polar icecaps are melting at an accelerated rate; there is flooding of vast areas and instability in climatic conditions now being witnessed all over the world.

Excessive rainfall causing unprecedented levels of flooding is of major concern, affecting many areas and turning them into disaster zones with all the misery for the inhabitants to endure, so it would not be inappropriate to spend a further moment or two looking at the effect which global warming can have on the situation.

A good place to start is to consider the analogy of what can happen within the home in a space such as a kitchen or bathroom where dampness is likely to prevail. As the process of cooking or whatever begins to take place in the usually warm atmosphere of the room, the air above the process begins to absorb more and more moisture until, moving about, it comes into contact with cooler surfaces like windows and external walls, upon which copious amounts of water are likely be deposited as condensation.

What happens on a global scale with normal rainfall is little different in principle from what takes place in the domestic environment. Warm air is able to absorb and retain more moisture than cooler air throughout the normal temperature range, so when warm heavily moisture-laden air is cooled by coming into contact with colder conditions it has to release the excess water which it can no longer retain at its lower temperature. This is nature at work.

Now, if due to global warming the air is raised to a

higher temperature than historically would have been the case, while passing over the land mass, it is then capable of picking up and absorbing even more moisture than hitherto while passing over the oceans; these possibly warmer, too, now will yield up even more of their moisture into the air, so compounding the problem. The overall position will hold good until the extra heavily moisture-laden air meets cooler conditions, upon which the extra moisture absorbed due to global warming will be deposited along with the normal level of precipitation.

Even a one degree Celsius rise above normal temperature in the atmosphere is likely to have a marked effect on rainfall, especially when one considers the vast amount of air above the oceans of the world capable of absorbing and later releasing copious amounts of excess moisture over the land from their elevated temperature.

The air around and above us is surely another of the wonders of God, of nature, and really qualifies for inclusion in the earlier chapters discussing our remarkable planet and universe. The air we breathe is invisible and its presence can so easily be taken for granted, but air has weight and, in the vastness of the atmosphere at the levels we dwell, something like every 13 cubic feet weighs one pound, which is the size of a cube 2.4 feet on all sides – much less than a cubic metre. While the air is still, at rest, all might seem well but when it begins to move then its weight, its mass, develops momentum which we experience as wind power, possibly leading to gales, storms and hurricanes which, when combined with low air pressure, have the effect of raising sea levels with the added risk of flooding on land.

So, what causes the air to move? Simply stated, it is because of the density and energy differences between the warmer and cooler air in the atmosphere, along with such other factors as the altitude of the air mass concerned and whether over land or water, also the rotation of the Earth. The effect of this is that higher and lower air pressure zones will develop, and it is a fact of nature that a higher pressure zone will tend to move towards one of a lower pressure, resulting in air movement.

At this stage one might well enquire why these nuggets of seemingly technical information have crept into this space, however interesting they may be. The answer – as has been said elsewhere – is because there is nothing new under the sun. Everything comes from God. The objective here is to illustrate that such natural behaviour of the elements, that in our time happens to comply with a branch of science described as physics, always existed. Always did, always does and always will.

Scientists and technocrats of our time have not themselves caused these things, and more, to happen. They always existed, whether or not understood by the people of bygone ages, though we remain unaware what past civilisations might have known. Discovery of all such phenomena in our time has been brought to our attention by an evolved process of learning, investigation, experiment and reason.

So, we hark back to the early part of this book, emphasising again the mysteries of this world which we mostly take for granted, presumably because they are all part of our natural environment and occur around us all the time. What needs to be kept in mind is that the legacy of everything that ever happened on this planet of a material nature, quite apart from the spiritual, remains with us.

Everything employed and happening in the service of humankind comes from finite existing sources – except, perhaps, the deposits and effects of an occasional comet wandering into our midst during the course of time. There are no other resources to call upon so it is our responsibility to conserve what we have until, maybe, we have access to other worlds. In these past few hundred years – and no more so than during this last century – Planet Earth has been plundered heavily to obtain possession of the natural resources bequeathed to us by its former inhabitants. Does this not sound like a possible result of excess population as well as the process of discovery?

During our stay on Planet Earth we all are its custodians and it is our bounden duty to leave it in a better shape than it was when we came into it, no matter how unimportant and insignificant we may consider ourselves to be and how small our contribution might be thought to be. This is the way ahead. Remember, all are equal in the sight of God!

Those who have conspired to ravage the earth and cause unwarranted and unacceptable despoliation will need to settle for their misguided actions on return to the world beyond depending on the level of personal responsibility. The deforestation of the rainforests, for example, the lungs of the planet which absorb CO_2 and release O_2; the incineration of the detritus to allow more cattle to graze, with the consequent increase all round in global temperature and greenhouse gases – are these not the result in part or whole of the needs for the population increase? The encouraging news is that there is no bar to making amends, even starting now.

The future is a reflection of the past, so if we cannot get things right now how can we contemplate a golden sunset for the years to come? If humankind were to embrace the understanding of reincarnation – future and past lives on earth – they might be more ready and willing to work towards a peaceful and comfortable planet readily prepared for their return to Earth in order to experience another stage in the journey of infinite life.

In the earlier chapter on Historical, Evolutionary & Spiritual Perspectives much emphasis was given to the remarkably short time in which our present civilisation appears to have woken from its slumber in order to get on with its progress and development into a scientific age. This is not what has really happened, of course, but it is a way of illustrating what little is known of life in the endless millennia stretching back before around 10,000 BC, and of the opportunities ahead if wise heads prevail.

There is little doubt that in this now rapidly changing and developing world, with all its attendant challenges and dangers, recourse to an understanding of the spiritual life, in which all human life is part, will give meaning to one's reason for being, for one's life on earth and the life eternal.

'It Always Was: Always Is: and Always Will Be'. It is, in fact, 'The Way Ahead'.

Guidance and leadership on Earth may well be coming from among the more recently born generations of older souls, and arrivals yet to appear – those who come into the world to help take humankind forward in whatever ways become necessary.

There has been a generous amount of discussion in esoteric circles during recent decades about the Indigo Children, the Crystal Children, the Rainbow Children and others of similar definitions who may follow. These will tend to be sensitive souls of advanced understanding who will be better left to find their own level in the world and not pushed too hard to fulfil the expectations of exhibited promise.

Acceptance and responsibility for situations of this kind lie very much with parents and teachers to begin with. We tell of a professional man who was keen to hear something about spiritual understanding; he listened attentively until mentioning that he had just become a father, upon which he was offered the news that his child might be an advanced soul. On hearing this his interest in the subject promptly ended.

To complete this projection of what the future might hold it is inevitably desirable to turn to the Bible. Revelations at the end of the Good Book has much to tell us in its interpretations, as do messages written on other pages for our benefit.

The disciples were asking Jesus, "What shall be the sign of thy coming, and of the end of the world?"

'And Jesus answered and said unto them, take heed that no man deceive you. For many shall come in my name, saying, I am Christ; and shall deceive many. And ye shall hear of wars and rumours of wars: see that ye not be troubled: for all these things must come to pass, but the end is not yet.

For nation shall rise against nation, and kingdom against kingdom: and there shall be famines, and pestilences, and earthquakes, in divers places.

All these are the beginning of sorrow.

And many false prophets shall rise, and shall deceive many And because iniquity shall abound, the love of many will wax cold. But he that shall endure unto the end, the same shall be saved.'

Matthew 24:3 (pt) 4 to 8, and 11 to 12. Mark 13:4 onward is like unto it.

The above message from the New Testament was spoken by Jesus around 2,000 years ago. From the Old Testament, Micah, a prophet in the time of Isaiah between 700 and 800 years earlier, almost 3,000 years ago, gave us this:

'But in the last days it shall come to pass, that the mountain of the house of the LORD shall be established in the top of the mountains, and it shall be exalted above the hills; and the people shall flow unto it.

And many nations shall come, and say, Come, and let us go up to the mountain of Lord, and to the house of the God of Jacob; and he will teach us of his ways, and we will walk in his paths: for the law shall go forth of Zion, and the word of the LORD from Jerusalem.

And he shall judge among many people, and rebuke strong nations afar off; and they shall beat their swords into plowshares, and their spears into pruning hooks; nation shall not lift up a sword against nation, neither shall they learn war any more.

But they shall sit every man under his vine and under his fig tree; and none shall make them afraid; for the mouth of the LORD of hosts hath spoken it.'

Micah 4:1 to 4

Any conclusions to be drawn from this chapter are well contained in the narrative. The main issue, however, is that by having been given freedom of choice, humankind is largely responsible for its own fate. There may be an overall guiding destiny but if the sensible pathway cannot be followed how can one complain? So, what needs to be remembered is that this is the 'Only Planet of Choice'; don't throw it away.

FOOTNOTE:

A discussion on 'The Future' might be thought to be incomplete without a word on futuristic travel to other worlds, as well as intervention into ours by interplanetary travellers. Such possibilities have been touched upon in chapter 5 and the likelihood of these cannot be ruled out no matter how far ahead; while remaining in the care, for the time being, of the capable hands of those engaged in astro-physics and space exploration; not to overlook those in the realms of intellectual science fiction. It is appropriate that speculation into this aspect of the future is not considered extensively in a treatise where the main concern is to explain the way forward for humankind on its spiritual pathway.

Nevertheless, part two of this chapter that follows gives an insight into what a more distant 'Future' might offer, based on suspected events, shrouded in mystery, coming from both the far and immediate past.

PART 2: DISTANT

The purpose of this guide has been to draw attention to the extraordinary, wonderful life and developmental opportunities available to all, regardless of personal religion, faith and belief. No matter how circumstances are explained, one will find that the many paths explored produce information of a fairly common understanding among those in spiritual, esoteric and psychic circles – differences, if any, being in the interpretation.

The Supreme Being is not only the God of all who worship in whatever manner and capacity that may be chosen but is also the deity of a religion we call science, and is a pragmatic God for those who seek the truth with respect and understanding for others.

There are references in the book to the possibility of earlier civilisations on our planet, as well as portals above the Earth to allow access for travellers coming from other realms.

There exists a yet unproven belief in the existence of two earlier civilisations, now long ceased, being those of Lemuria and Atlantis. Lemuria was the earlier of the two and is reckoned to have had a population of a lesser developed human life. Atlantis followed with a more advanced culture but was destroyed eventually due to an unacceptable and dangerous form of living: becoming literally blown apart. Does that not offer a thought for concern in our present era where nations exist with trigger fingers over the buttons of weapons primed to bring about nuclear annihilation?

Fortunately for later civilisations, in the story of Atlantis, it was only the land mass of that country that took the full force of the explosion and not the whole planet. What remained is said to have disappeared beneath a great sea of water which was to become the Atlantic Ocean. Other locations are suggested from time to time, one such being in the Mediterranean.

But in the Atlantic nearer to Florida there is or was the Bermuda Triangle, an area in which aircraft and ships have disappeared, and then Roswell further west on solid ground where there was a report of an alien craft crashing, denied by the authorities, similar to the manner in which the case of the missing aircraft was explained away. Could these happenings have occurred in areas having access portals in the sky above through which extra terrestrial visitors could come and go?

There is speculation in the story of Atlantis that some survivors, their successors or maybe spiritual beings from the vanished continent appeared later in the early days of Egyptian life, bringing with them a knowledge of some of the ancient mysteries from the lost land.

The events affecting both civilisations could have taken

place over a vast amount of time. The Egyptian scene could have opened up around 12,000 years ago with the arrival of the first Atlanteans who over a period of time would have been able to set about developing the basis for a society, possibly leading to that of an order which there is to this day. This will have been around a time at the end of the last ice age when the more primitive Britons and others would have been coming in from the cold.

The rise and fall of these two earlier civilisations will not necessarily be the only ones to be considered, as it might be assumed they took place just within the last million years. Even if they had spanned a period greater than that the probability is that it will still have been of small magnitude when set against 4,560 million years of the planet's existence. So, there has been plenty of opportunity in earlier millennia for other societies to become firmly established.

In the matter of portals over the Earth there is a theory that there are openings in the space above the planet through which space travellers from other worlds have been able to visit us since time immemorial, these openings tending to possess very high energy, each maybe in the form of a vortex above a place of high spiritual activity. By this means, incoming visitors of higher intelligence would have been able to seed those conceived in Lemuria, leading to an increased level of awareness. There could have been a similar situation in Atlantis and Egypt, the degree of intelligence improving all the while.

The purpose for the bestowal of increasing intelligence on humankind is to assist its spiritual evolution, moving forward all the while. It is the gift of the Creator for everyone to use as they wish. During the countless ages of collective development on other worlds, mankind here has repeatedly failed to grasp the significance or has turned his back on the God-given individualistic opportunities laid before him, preferring to indulge with myopic vision in greed, power, wars, unspeakable cruelty and bestiality right up to this time. Our ultimate home is with God in whose image we are made. It is possible for all to become closer to Him as personal evolution and corresponding frequency of vibration merges with the standards obtained in the higher echelons of the spiritual levels.

Planet Earth is designated as a sphere of natural beauty allowing its inhabitants to be free thinkers with freedom of choice. It is, in fact, the only planet of choice, and more so when reckoned against those which came earlier. The way ahead beckons, the opportunities are there for the taking – why not grasp them now!

TAILPIECE:

To emphasise a point made above: many moons after this chapter was written, heard on a late night intellectual television broadcast, two otherwise learned men were in discussion, one interviewing the other.

One said, "Science will replace God." The other agreed enthusiastically

How little is understood! 'God IS Science', 'Science IS God'.

This kind of discussion follows similar current pseudo scientific talk that superior artificial intelligence will take over from man, who will then be unable to do anything about it.

If this should be a likelihood, which it isn't, it would be none other than the fault of scientists for devising and creating such possibilities over which they would no longer be able to exercise complete control; akin to that of nuclear power. As discussed earlier, do not blame God for the mistakes of man, although those who watch over Planet Earth in the name of God will be there to step in should the tipping point be reached. We are by no means alone in the universe; on the contrary, as a very special planet in the heavens we are watched over most carefully to ensure the preservation of all that there is.

30

ROUND-UP

This is very much like the earlier chapter, 'The Bottom Line' but seen as it were from the other end of a telescope. That is, looking back on some of what's been discussed in a nutshell, a form of recapitulation, a quick run-through. Fuller information needs to be read, of course, in the relevant chapters. Topics from one chapter may be amalgamated with or become part of another, supplementary information may be added, here and there, and different expressions used – almost a second helping.

Having explained the bizarre events which brought us to put pen to paper we eulogised on the incredible breathtaking beauty and enormity of space – the cosmos – as well as the virtually indigestible age of Planet Earth, of which we know so little except for comparatively recent times. God's hand was surely at work; and were there civilisations before ours? There was plenty of time for that to be possible; and was humankind seeded from angel beings and visiting space travellers? What other reason might there be for the marked separation in the Evolution of Humankind from that of the Primates?

We touched on the Reality of Spirituality. While reverence and respect are called for at all times, as should always be the case in a society that prides itself on its culture, the suggestion is that by being relaxed in the knowledge that Spiritual Life around us is very much a part of our everyday existence, we are aided in an understanding of why we are here on Planet Earth.

Energy and vibrations tell us that everything vibrates according to its particular level of energy, and that includes both the physical and the spiritual, except that the frequency of vibration in the spirit body operates at a higher level than that of the physical, which means it can pass though matter unseen. The higher frequency of vibration developed in human beings occasioned by their way of life and other circumstances will be of untold help when passing over.

The Seven Levels informs us that with Earth as the lowest level of habitat for the human spirit there are six more levels in the Light for the spirit to ascend in the vastness of time and space after completing any number of lives (incarnations) on Earth. The Seven Levels are sometimes described as the Planes of Ascension.

Reincarnation, once understood and accepted by the early Church, follows on from what has just been stated. Any idea that we have but one life, and that is all, needs be adjusted to take into account the repeated journeys to be made to the Light and back again for further lives on Earth until we have evolved spiritually to a level permitting a place in the higher levels. The progress depends on us; there are no shortcuts, it's just a matter of application. This concept links in with that of vibrational development to facilitate our going forward. Each return to Earth permits an opportunity to agree on one's parents and, hence, birthplace, probably from one's larger soul family.

Karma: The Law of Cause and Effect, The Golden Rule. 'Do unto others what you would have done to yourself.' Otherwise the process of Reincarnation will bring one back to Earth time and time again until by one's own efforts all the misdeeds have been expunged – and there may be periods spent in the Lower Astral in the process.

Because the use of the terms Soul and Spirit appear to be so interchangeable in everyday use, a guide to their truer meanings is offered. The Soul can be likened to a mantle encapsulating the body holistic in life then continuing in its everlasting and real self when liberated at the time of passing over. The Spirit, containing the Mind, accompanies the Soul and provides the vital spark for its animation. The Soul and Spirit, with what are styled the Subtle Bodies, are associated with the physical during Earthly life.

Different models, but with a similarity of approach to the concept of Subtle Bodies, are used to illustrate the significance of their working relationship with the human body. Starting close to the Physical body and moving outward in layers, we depict the intangible cloaking bodies of the Etheric, Astral, Mental, Intuitive, Soul and Spirit. The aura is not classified here as a Subtle Body, it being a manifestation of one's Spiritual Energy. The Higher and Lower Selves are mentioned, they being our lifelong connections with Heaven and Earth.

At the time of the Passing Over when 'the silver cord is loosed' it is the physical body that experiences Death, having fulfilled its function for the present stay on Earth, now completed. The soul and spirit, along with the mind, enter the world of Spirit, containing the fund of knowledge, wisdom and experience gathered over any number of incarnations. Upon returning to Earth, which is more often the case, the incoming soul/spirit – the eternal 'you' – will have settled beforehand on the choice of new parents and, consequently, where they will be located. Spiritual lore has it that part of the spirit will enter the imminent birth at the moment of conception, with increasing input over the early years of life.

All being well at the time of passing over, the spirit will enter the celestial Light and be accommodated on one of the many levels, usually the second level to begin with as Planet Earth is classed as the first level. The intensity and brilliance of the Light will be overwhelmingly powerful while remaining exceptionally welcoming. Those who have had near death experiences speak of their reluctance to return to Earth.

The Electromagnetic Spectrum is another example of God's hand at work, providing as it does a technological illustration of cosmic energy and rays of light which are part of our everyday environment. This is wandering on to the field of science – just another small way to show how physical science and spiritual science come together, except that it is the spiritual science which leads: 'as above, so below'; if only mainstream science could recognise this!

The Eternal Pathway illustrates how we are all on the everlasting slope, onward and upward through countless incarnations until ultimate entry into the upper echelons of Light. There is no hurry, just a constant and repetitious journey to get things right over aeons of time (Earth time). One does slip, perhaps, now and again, which means a return visit to go through that lifetime again, and if one's actions have been truly reprehensible it could mean a spell or two in the Lower Astral until one is able to move forward again according to one's own efforts. The entire journey can be a very long process. Not to be overlooked also are those who deny belief in the life hereafter and so can find themselves wandering around in limbo after passing, as in a state of confusion, they are unable to understand and accept why they are in a sort of 'no man's land' between Heaven and Earth.

Religious Considerations and the Belief System may be coupled here as they represent the desire of the individual to accept or reject God's Holy Ordinance which is there for their benefit now or later, and to which the doubters and disbelievers will eventually find themselves turning, or returning, so why delay the inevitable? Experience God's munificent grace now.

Prayer to some is a very personal matter. Suggestions have been made for anyone who has difficulty in opening up in this way. Prayer can be a means of asking for a blessing for yourself or others, or for asking for your needs – but not your wants. Jesus invites one to pray privately and quietly when you can, though this is not easy when among others doing likewise in assemblies. Prayer can be efficacious in a passive capacity in the healing process, differing from spiritual 'hands-on' healing where the healer has an active role. Individual, group or guided Meditation helps to still the mind and assists with concentration and spiritual progress.

It is axiomatic that when the chips are down and everything is turning negative, one turns to God. But when the picture is rosy there may be a tendency to get on with the more pressing events; God is always there; He will be there again tomorrow or the day after when there will be more time available or a more cogent reason to turn to Him. There is no better form of insurance than a policy taken out with God. If one stays that much closer to Him when in the sunny uplands, He is more likely to hear your call no matter how faint when the dark clouds roll in and despair is all around. True, He will not let you down when you cry out in distress even if you have abandoned Him, but always remember one has a choice, a benefit granted to those on this planet. If the action of that choice born out of the freewill gifted to humankind causes distress and mayhem to self and others, there is little point in bemoaning, "Where's God?"

The Holy Bible is a sacred and historic chronicle which people have paid with their lives to bring to us, as well as to possess and read for themselves. It is upon swearing an oath on the Bible that one's word is held to be sacrosanct. The Good Book contains much beneficial advice and wisdom, which can be read in the English language of the 17th century or from translations in the modern vernacular, quotations from the former appearing throughout this book.

Self-empowerment means that by and large we all have the power to change things ourselves, for ourselves.

To change our lives forever and for the better. The key to unlock that trunk full of the ancient wisdom which is stored in the attic of our mind lies within us. The opportunity, the ability, is with us, not with the 'other person' who we might well like to call upon to do it for us and thereby relieve us of responsibility. Remember, 'Energy follows Thought'. We are what we think we are, and we can change that view of ourselves for the better if needed.

Present-day Mediumship has come a long way in the past century. Gone are the days of the séance; lighter and more gentle approaches now prevail since connection with the world beyond has entered mainstream and become more transparent, though it may still be possible for the old ways to pop up here and there. The Bible, a book of inestimable spiritual value, has mediumship within its pages, of both spiritual and psychic forms. The spiritual leads and the psychic follows. Different styles of the practice are given in the appropriate chapter. While one can be comfortable and relaxed when participating in the process, we emphasise that it is not an art, science or pastime in which to be dabbling. Unless one is competent to an acceptable level, no matter how gifted it is imperative that one seeks and works with qualified personnel.

Pure Spiritual Healing may rightly be described as the quintessence of Mediumship, and of the spiritual form, as distinct from that of the psychic. The healer as an instrument of God operates as a channel to conduct the healing rays-energy-power from the source in the celestial spheres to the intended recipients wherever located. Responsible healers will not wish to claim credit for themselves, knowing that their accomplishments are as a result of a gift from God, with the benefit of discovery, learning and experience. Healers registered with an established healing group or organisation should operate according to a code of ethics which forbids the promise or guarantee to heal or cure any specific affliction, condition or adversity. It is the will of the Lord which prevails in all circumstances. As touched upon earlier, healing organisations and practising healers have their own particular ways of dealing with the healing process, so their views may differ from what is expressed here.

Astonishing acts of natural healing and psychic ability as reported at the top of the front page of a leading Sunday newspaper in 1935 might well have been considered truly amazing by the readership of that time. Unlike many customs and practices almost taken for granted these days, there would have been a widespread lack of knowledge and understanding, as well as taboos; this being prior to our more enlightened age, for which we have to thank the gifted ones who came to show the way forward after the Second World War. But as the news item was from a time before the opening up of a new age of understanding, it can be said that there is nothing new under the sun; we remember, too, that spiritual and psychic interests were re-establishing themselves in the 19th century, and Jesus led the way supremely two thousand years ago.

If one chooses to train for any profession or discipline there are inevitably ground rules to learn, and in many instances these may be for one's own safety and protection. In responsible countries no one is permitted to be in charge of a motor vehicle before demonstrating an ability to control the machine without being a danger to one's self or others. Such is the case when operating in the field of bona fide parapsychology, where Grounding and Protection is an essential part of the training. Needless to say, attempts to work in these areas without prior instruction and supervision from those with knowledge and experience is not to be recommended.

We have talked about love, meaning Unconditional Love for all sentient beings, and when one looks at the chart showing the Kingdoms of God it amounts to an impressive list of those to whom the universal love of humankind is to be extended. It goes well beyond the human line and into that of the animal, mineral and plant domains, and even into the world of Spirit where, for example, we spoke earlier of our sadness when humankind takes pleasure in deriving fun at the expense of Earthbound and trapped spirits – so-called 'ghost hunting'.

Elements of society appear to be so heavily engaged as never before in a desire for a mix of power, material progress and wealth, with all that becomes encompassed in the train of these goals, that there is a paramount need for balance in all areas of life. This has been never more so than in this still young 21st century, in which the rate of change compared with earlier centuries is happening at such an unimaginable pace with every indication that it will become even faster. What we know of our past on this planet has recorded little in the way of progress as measured in current terms until relatively recent times and there is no evidence to suggest that this will abate short of a cataclysm.

When deep consideration is given to the future of this beautiful planet there are undoubtedly many issues of concern, balanced always, of course, against the inspirations, endeavours, actions and hopes of all who strive to live and work peacefully alongside those who govern wisely. A particular problem which will assuredly need to be addressed is that of population explosion throughout the globe. It would not be unrealistic to ask who should be dealing with a problem of this kind, God or Man? Unless this is part of a greater plan for Earth – which seems most unlikely – it is man's responsibility, as with all the vexing matters of similar concern, to get his house in order while the opportunity permits.

This is the message from part one of 'Future Considerations' – the more immediate concerns.

The future offers a clear warning of what might befall the planet if it does not get its act together, especially as there is now increasing belief that we are not by any means the first civilisation to have occupied this space, the knowledge we command being scant when set against the backdrop of the globe's immensely long history. On the other hand, the outlook can be regarded in a more optimistic light if all the people of all the nations work together to save the world and all that dwells therein from going over the brink. It is essentially 'A Matter of Choice'.

This is the message from part two of 'Future Considerations' – the more distant – which can too easily reflect the ways of the past; but we are not alone. It would not be unreasonable to assume that even now our planet is being watched and that visitors from space are ever more likely to appear in time to come.

ABOUT THE AUTHOR

Born and named William George Thomas in the year 1924 at home in Bloomsbury, Central London, the one-time literary area bounded by High Holborn to the south, Euston Road and Kings Cross to the north, Grays Inn Road to the east and Tottenham Court Road to the west.

A most interesting area for a young person to be raised and be connected to for the first 26 years of life with all there was to be seen and understood that might aid personal development. From the British Museum on the doorstep, the great steam railway stations, Regency squares and nearby Covent Garden (old fruit/vegetable market and opera house), the West End theatres, the old City of London, great business houses, activity on the River Thames, and so much more. Family connections were generally local and strong, and there was a good deal of activity outside the homes on a level difficult to envisage now with present-day security considerations, the distractions of the internet, television, and the like; but it was the way of life then.

The '20s and '30s were halcyon days and then came the war, declared a few months before entering the '40s. With schools and their pupils being evacuated from the capital by the authorities at the outset, and having savoured that dubious experience in the obviously considered safe haven of Luton, an industrial town a scarce 30 miles from the centre of the metropolis, Geoff (as he was later to be dubbed) returned to London after six weeks to remain there throughout the conflict, sharing and absorbing the sights, sounds and happenings in the wartime capital.

With the dearth of regular schooling in London at the time, Geoff entered into an indentured student apprenticeship with a leading engineering company operating in the construction industry, which provided hands-on training and part-time college education, all leading to academic and professional qualifications. During wartime this meant being involved in the design and construction of aspects of munitions factories, military establishments, airfields and the like, a form of service described then as 'war work' for everybody: men and women not in the armed services but voluntarily or compulsorily engaged in contributing to the war effort.

His wartime service contract coming to an end in September 1945, Geoff was called to the colours in mid-1946 and spent two years in the Corps of Royal Engineers, including time at the Royal School of Military Engineering under a War Office posting at Brompton, adjacent to Chatham in Kent. It was during a training period elsewhere that he contracted a serious ear infection passed on by a fellow soldier, the result being that after fulfilling his service period he was awarded the King's Badge for Loyal Service, granted to those who sustained disabilities of one kind or another.

After leaving the army he soon took up a position in an engineering company engaged in similar work to that in which he had previously trained. Moving at a steady pace he began to acquire increasingly senior positions in various companies, going through managerial roles up to that of managing director. In 1967 he formed a small private engineering and consultancy practice together with a former technical director he had trained. His most able business-trained wife of 17 years was enlisted to handle the financial and administrative duties. This lasted 25 years, until retirement.

It was at what is now the Victory Services Club in London that he met Jacqueline in 1949; she had volunteered and served towards the end of the war and afterwards in the Women's Royal Naval Service, the Wrens, having joined at the earliest age permitted. They had both served time in the Chatham area but were not to come across each other until after demobilisation. A year later, on St Swithin's day 1950, they were married in Christ Church in Woburn Square, Bloomsbury, where Christina Rossetti, a devout Anglican and English poet, had been buried. Alas, the church no longer exists, having been demolished later to make way for more building space to meet the requirements of the expanding London University.

Bloomsbury, just like the rest of London and the whole country, had churches, which now are either non-existent or declared redundant. Regent Square had two grand churches at opposing ends, one being known as the 'Scotch Church', the busy and main Presbyterian church in London, and the other the Anglican church, St Peter's, where Geoff was to be baptised and attend. His sister was at the 'Scotch Church'.

It was a happy time at St Peter's, not too well attended in such a diverse area but having an enthusiastic core of young people eagerly participating in the liturgical, social and youth activities, including the Scout movement, all on offer. By the age of 12, having been in the choir for a while, Geoff, or William as known then, was an acolyte serving at the right hand of the priest at the high altar.

Then on return from Scout camp in August 1939 everything changed abruptly; the nation was on a war footing, and from that time the accustomed way of life was gone, never to be the same again. His college was preparing for the evacuation of students; eligible young men of military age were being served with their 'call-up' papers. Practice air raid precautions started, streets being 'blacked out' (darkened at night), and then on 3rd September 1939 Britain declared war and the conflagration was on.

Friendships managed to hold together for most of the first year until the bombing started, resulting in friends and families being dispersed due to the destruction of lives and property. Neighbourhood friends were killed in air raids, relocation of housing became a regular feature, and then St Peter's Church was damaged by bomb blast to the extent that while being able to continue for a while on a substantially reduced basis it was eventually demolished.

The site of the nearby Presbyterian 'Scotch Church' was also affected by wartime bombing, including that from a V2 rocket falling on a relative's dwelling nearby. This church, too, was demolished and subsequently rebuilt in the Chelsea area. The V1 flying bombs, which preceded the silent rockets, were well recognised by the sound of their motors until the cut-off point when silence prevailed as they dropped to earth.

Events happening during and immediately after the war began to direct Geoff towards an early interest in the spiritual life. In 1943 a close friend in the RAF was killed in a raid over the continent and two years later another lost his life in a flying accident in South Wales, not long before the end of hostilities in Europe. These incidents began to find him questioning the totality of death, for rational and not emotional reasons; this being prior to a visit to a leading spiritual centre of the day, where the medium in charge invited him to join their circle as he was 'mediumistic'. The matter rested there, however, for the while, as the time had now come for military service.

There is a turning point in many a person's lifetime brought about by any number of reasons, some inconceivably bizarre, others personal or of family shock situations, as was the case for Geoff and Jacqueline when their only son, Matthew, took ill at the age of 17, this proving to be a lasting condition.

Due to what might well have been a nudge from the other side – the world beyond – Geoff found himself looking deeper into this event and, with his spiritual questioning retained from years earlier, was soon involved in a serious pursuit for a closer understanding of the purpose of life. Starting in 1986 and for the following six years he entered into a form of study and practice with leading specialist practitioners and teaching organisations of the time, among which included The College of Psychic Studies, The College of Healing, the National Federation of Spiritual Healers, and others, e.g. Morley College – Counselling, and City Literary Institute – Teaching Adult Learners, all leading to appropriate qualifications.

He was awarded a Diploma from The College of Healing in 1990, of which he then became an Associate (ACOH), followed by full Membership (MCOH) in 1993. In the same year he became a Healer Member of the National Federation of Spiritual Healers (later designated MNFSH). Around the turn of the century he participated in the early days of Spirit Release organisations, and in 2008 he received certification as a Recognised Medium with the Christian Spiritualist Society International.

From 1992 to 1997 he had his own healing centre in Fulham, from where he became the visiting healer to a GP's surgery for a period of five years. In 1995, by permission of the rector and Church authorities, he founded what was to become The Healing Fellowship at St Mary-le-Bow in Cheapside in the City of London. This has lasted over 20 years, during which time there have been around 1,000 meetings involving about 10,000 attendances from those coming forward to receive healing and/or instruction in spiritual healing and spiritual development. Some members from training courses have gone on to become significant practitioners and therapists.

Quoting from information previously included in an in-house publication: Geoff Thomas is a born healer and medium, as he was first led to understand when a very young man but was not to appreciate fully on a conscious level until after serving a spell in the Army followed by a career as a professional engineer/businessman in which he has been as much at home on the workshop floor and construction site as within the board room.

'With the added benefit of having a background of science and technology, Geoff has the clear ability to perceive the relationship between happenings which occur beyond the comprehension of admitted scientific understanding and the spiritual influences and cosmic forces which bring them about, knowing that the unexplained or paranormal on one level of existence is but the normal on the higher planes of realisation.'

Geoff gradually retired from engineering practice in the 1990s, retaining professional connections, being a Chartered Engineer (C Eng) and a Fellow of several leading institutes. He is on the alumni of the London South Bank University (LSBU). After almost 60 years of marriage, Jacqueline passed on in 2009; their son – Matthew – is in Bristol, not too far from Gloucestershire where Geoff divides his time with Greater London.

THE LORD'S PRAYER

Our Father which art in heaven, Hallowed be thy Name
Thy kingdom come, Thy will be done, in earth as it is in
Heaven. Give us this day our daily bread; And forgive us
our trespasses, As we forgive them that trespass against us;
And lead us not into temptation, But deliver us from evil.
For thine is the kingdom, the power and the glory,
For ever and ever. Amen.

> From the Book of Common Prayer,
> Taken from the words of Lord Jesus, in
> The King James Bible, Matthew 6:9-13

AN EVENING PRAYER

Lighten our darkness, we beseech thee, O LORD;
And by thy great mercy defend us from all perils
And dangers of this night; for the love of thy only
Son, our Saviour Jesus Christ. Amen.

From the Book of Common Prayer

BIBLIOGRAPHY

Where two dates are given against a title of a book, the first is that of the original publication or issue and the second is that of the edition to which this bibliography refers. Some of the titles currently circulating may have later dates of release, while others may have been transferred to an alternative publisher or be out of print.

Alder, Vera Stanley: *The Initiation of the World*: Samuel Weiser: 1939/2000

Amorah Quan Yin: *Pleiadian Perspectives on Human Evolution*: Bear and Company: 1996

Andrews, Ted: *The Occult Christ*: Dragonhawk Publishing: 2006

Ash, David & Hewitt, Peter: *Science of the Gods*: Gateway Books: 1990

Atwater LHD, PMH: *Beyond the Indigo Children*: Bear and Company: 2005

Barbanell, Maurice: *Light from Silver Birch*: compiled by Pam Riva: The Spiritual Truth Press: 1983/1999

Besant, Maisie: *Akhenaten Speaks. The Nature of Spiritual Healing*: Eye of Gaza Press: 1991

Beatty, Mabel: *The White Brotherhood Man Made Perfect – The Science of Spiritual Evolution*: Rider 1927/Pelegrin Trust – Pilgrim Books 1987

Bek, Lilla with Pullar, Phillipa: *To The Light*: Unwin Hyman Limited: 1985/1987

Bek, Lilla, and Pullar, Phillipa: *The Seven Levels of Healing*: Century Hutchinson (Rider). Foreword by Don Copland

Binder, Otto O & Flindt, Max H: *We Are The Children Of The Stars*: Fawcett Publications: 1974/Hampton Roads Publishing Company, Inc: 2013

Bloom, William: *Devas, Fairies and Angels – A Modern Approach*: Gothic Image: 1986

Brennan, Barbara Ann: *Hands of Light*: Bantam Books: 1987/1988

Burl, Aubrey: *Stone Circles of Britain, Ireland and Brittany*: Yale University Press: 1995

Byrne, Michael & Bush, GR (Editors): *St Mary-le-Bow, A History*: Wharncliffe Books: 2007

Cooke, Grace: *White Eagle on Reincarnation*: White Eagle Publishing Trust: 2006

Cooke, Grace: *Wisdom from White Eagle*: White Eagle Publishing Trust: 1967/1991

Cooke, Grace: *Spiritual Unfoldment*: White Eagle Publishing Trust: Four Volumes – 1942/1944; (2) 1969/1989; (3) 1987;) (4) 1988

Cooke, Grace: *Memories of Incarnation*: White Eagle Publishing Trust: 2006

Couper, Heather and Henbest, Nigel: *Space Encyclopaedia*: Dorling Kindersley: 1999

Edwards, Harry: *A Guide to the Understanding and Practice of Spiritual Healing*: The Healer Publishing Company Limited: 1974

Essene, Virginia: *New Teachings for a Wakening Humanity- the Christ*: Spiritual Education Endeavour: 1986/1987

Fiore, Dr Edith: *The Unquiet Dead*: Ballantine Books (Random House): 1987

Graves, Tom: *Pendulum Dowsing*: The Elements of: Element Books Limited: 1989

Gittings, Fred: *Encyclopaedia of the Occult*: Rider: 1986

Greaves, Helen: *Testimony of Light*: Rider/Random House: 1969/2005: Reprinted by Churches' Fellowship for Psychical and Spiritual Studies (CFPSS)

Hickman, DO, Irene: *Remote Depossession*: Hickman Systems: 1994/1997

Hislop, Dr John S: *Seeking Divinity*: Sri Sathya Sai Baba: Sri Sathya Sai Books & Publications Trust: 1998/2007

Lawrence, Roy: *The Practice of Christian Healing*: Triangle, SPCK: 1996/1998

Lilly, Simon: *Healing with Crystals*: Anness Publishing Limited (Southwater): 2001

Marciniak, Barbara: *Bringers of the Dawn, Teachings from the Pleiadians*: Bear & Company Inc; 1948/1992

Meehan, Bridget: *The Healing Power of Prayer*: Society for Promoting Christian Knowledge: (GB): 1988/1996

Neate, Tony: *The Guide Book*: Gateway Book 1986/Pegasus Foundation 1991

Neate, Tony: *H-A, On Life and Living*: Pegasus Foundation: 1992

Neate, Tony: *H-A, New Dimensions in Healing*: Eye of Gaza Press: 1999/2007

Neate, Tony: *Channelling for Everyone*: Piatkus: 1997/2012

Newman, Hugh: *Earth Grids*: Wooden Books Ltd: 2008/2010

Northage, Ivy: *Mediumship Made Simple*: The Psychic Press: 1986/The College of Psychic Studies: 1994

Northage, Ivy & Chan: *Spiritual Realisation*: Pelegrin Trust: 1998

Northage, Ivy & Chan: *Journey Beyond*: Psychic Press: 1972/1988

Northage, Ivy & Chan: *Light of the World*: Spiritualist Association of Great Britain: 1999

Nowotny, Dr Karl & Grete: *Messages from a Doctor in the Fourth Dimension*: Six Volumes – (1) 1972/1976; (2) 1972/1992; (3) 1972/1993; (4) 1972/1994; (5) 1973/1995; (6) 1972/1996: Dr Karl Nowotny Foundation e. V English Edition

Noyes, Ralph (Editor) & Taylor, Busty (Photographs): *The Crop Circle Enigma*: Gateway Books: 1990

Origen: *On First Principles*: Butterworth GW (Translation): Christian Classics, Ave Maria Press, Inc: 2013

Polge, Coral with Hunter, Kay: *Living Images; The Story of a Psychic Artist*: Regency Press: 1985/Spiritual Association of Great Britain: 1997

Reccia, Michael G: *The Joseph Communications*, The Fall: Band of Light Media Limited: 2012

Roberts, Ursula: *Hints on Mediumistic Development*: Psychic Press Ltd: 1987/1990

Rulof, Jozef: *The Cycle of the Soul*: Wayti Publishers Empe – the Netherlands: 1st Ed 1938

Rulof, Jozef: *The Origin of the Universe*: Wayti, Apeldoorn: 1st English edition: 2000

Rulof, Jozef: *A View into the Hereafter*: Three Volumes: 1st English editions: 2000

Schlemmer, Phyllis: *The Only Planet of Choice*: The Council of Nine, Essential Briefings from Deep Space: Gateway Books: 1993/1997

Sharland, Margaret: *The Wisdom of Red Cloud*: M Sharland Publications: 2014

Stock, Victor: *Taking Stock, Confessions of a City Priest*: Harper Collins Publishers: 2001

Stringer, Chris & Peter Andrews: *The Complete World of Human Evolution*: Thames & Hudson: 2005/Second edition 2012

Young, Alan: *Spiritual Healing, Miracle or Mirage*: DeVorss & Company: 1981/1986

Weiss, Dr Brian: *Many Lives, Many Masters*: Piatkus: 1998/1994

Woodard, Christopher: *A Doctor Heals by Faith*: Max Parrish and Co, Ltd: 1953/1955

And always:
The Holy Bible and the Book of Common Prayer, or the sacred books of one's own denomination

INDEX

C

exceptionally important event in
121–2
glossolalia in 122–3
hidden messages 120
huge amount of knowledge
within 120–1
mediumship within 214
nature of 117, 213
production and existence of 117
psychic activity within 121
stories handed down 117–18
translations 118–19, 213
versions 119
Holy Ghost 71, 122, 134
Holy Trinity 41, 43, 99, 103
Homo sapiens 25–6, 30
Hospitals 56, 64
hour clock 32, 34–5
humanism 101
humans
comparatively short history
27–9, 36
emergence of 25–6
evolution 38–9
'our time' 24–5, 31–7, 39
Hunt, William Holman 85–6

displaying anger 179–80
dying upon cross 117–18
future projections 200–1
Lord's Prayer 225
on prayer 212
on questioning God 104
time of 34–5
on unconditional love 175–6
John the Baptist 99

Karma
'Akashic Records' 68
ambiguity starting point 65–6
aspect of positive 68
biblical evidence of 68–9
as cornerstone of spiritual life 43
definition 66, 187
Eastern tradition's intention 66
example 66–7
Great Lords of 68
inability to remember past lives 67
justice 68
karmic debts 69
law of cause and effect 65, 210
on Planet Earth 67–8
Sanskrit word from India 51
Kingdoms of God 18, 178, 181–2, 216

I

ice into steam 47
Indigo Children 50, 200
infants 81–2
interplanetary travel 29–30, 184, 202
Intuitive body 75–6, 210
Intuitive level 57–8
Isfahan, Persia 59

J

January to December countdown 36
Jesus
acts of healing 99, 158
on Celestial Light 85–86

L

law of cause and effect 65, 210
Lemuria 204–5
'letting go' 109, 111, 178
Lewis, Mark 6, 157
ley lines 28–9
life and death paradox 10–11
life, meaning of 11, 36–7
Light see Celestial Light; Realm of
Light
'Light of the World' artwork 85–6
lighting
artificial 87–9
from candles 87–8, 90
natural 87